Animals in the Rain Forest

By John Wood

KidHaven
PUBLISHING

Published in 2018 by
KidHaven Publishing, an Imprint of Greenhaven Publishing, LLC
353 3rd Avenue
Suite 255
New York, NY 10010

Designer: Matt Rumbelow
Editor: Holly Duhig

Cataloging-in-Publication Data

Names: Wood, John.
Title: Animals in the rain forest / John Wood.
Description: New York : KidHaven Publishing, 2018. | Series: Where animals live | Includes index.
Identifiers: ISBN 9781534523777 (pbk.) | 9781534523753 (library bound) | ISBN 9781534525139 (6 pack) | ISBN 9781534523760
(ebook)
Subjects: LCSH: Rain forest animals–Juvenile literature.
Classification: LCC QL112.W66 2018 | DDC 591.734–dc23

Printed in the United States of America

3 5944 00140 0793

CPSIA compliance information: Batch #CW18KL: For further information contact Greenhaven Publishing LLC, New York, New York at 1-844-317-7404.

Please visit our website, www.greenhavenpublishing.com. For a free color catalog of all our
high-quality books, call toll free 1-844-317-7404 or fax 1-844-317-7405.

Photo credits: Abbreviations: l-left, r-right, b-bottom, t-top, c-center, m-middle.
2 – Curioso. 3 – Twinsterphoto. 4 – MarcusVDT. 5: tl – Daniel Etzold; mc – Dudarev Mikhail; mr – Zephyr_p; bl – Ilyshev Dmitry; br – Piotr Krzeslak.
6 – Galyna Andrushko. 7 – Ammit Jack. 8 – Gustavo Frazao. 9: tl – Kjersti Joergensen; mr – fototrips; bl – Dr Morley Read. 10 – RAJU SONI. 11 –
dangdumrong. 12 – Dr Morley Read. 13 – khlungcenter. 14 – Sharp. 15 – Vladimir Wrangel. 16 – Michael Lynch. 17 – belizar. 18 – Ryan M. Bolton. 19
-Vladimir Wrangel. 20 – Rich Carey. 21 – Rich Carey. 22 – Sergey Uryadnikov. 23 – reptiles4all.
Images are courtesy of Shutterstock.com, with thanks to Getty Images, Thinkstock Photo, and iStockphoto.

CONTENTS

Words that look like this can be found in the glossary on page 24.

WHAT IS A

HABITAT?

A habitat is a place where an animal lives. It provides the animal with food, shelter, and everything else it needs to survive.

4

There many different habitats in the world. Each one is home to several different animals.

mountains

oceans

The Arctic

deserts

forests

5

WHAT IS A
RAIN FOREST?

A rain forest is another word for a jungle. Rain forests grow in hot countries near the equator, where it rains often. This means the weather is wet and warm.

rain forest

The biggest rain forest in the world is the Amazon rain forest in South America. It is home to many plants and animals that aren't found anywhere else in the world.

The Amazon rain forest

The Amazon

South America

RAIN FOREST HABITAT

There are many types of rain forest habitat. Some animals live in the treetops while some live on the forest floor.

8

Other animals live in the thick layer of trees called the rain forest canopy. Rivers that run through rain forests also provide a habitat for many animals.

treetops

rain forest canopy

forest floor

BENGAL TIGERS

Bengal tigers are one of the biggest animals in the rain forest. They live on the forest floor. When hunting their prey, tigers hide among small plants.

Tigers like to make the whole rain forest their home. They roam around, climbing trees and swimming in rivers.

Every tiger has a different pattern of stripes.

LEAF-CUTTER ANTS

Leaf-cutter ants live in nests underground in a big group called a colony. There can be over one million ants in a single colony.

The ants carry leaves from rain forest trees back to their home under the forest floor. Fungus grows on the leaves which the ants eat later.

SLOTHS

One of the many animals that live in the rain forest canopy is the sloth. Sloths spend most of their lives hanging in trees and moving slowly.

sloth

Sometimes, small insects and algae live and grow in the sloth's fur. This makes the sloth look green, which helps them to hide from predators in the green canopy.

VAMPIRE BATS

Vampire bats live high up in the treetops. When they aren't flying, bats generally hang upside down.

Bats sleep during the day and hunt at night.

They hunt by sneaking up on sleeping animals and drinking a small amount of their blood. Most of the time, the animals don't even wake up.

GREEN ANACONDAS

Green anacondas are the heaviest snakes in the world. They spend most of their time in rivers and swamps, where they can move quickly.

The anaconda's scales make it hard for them to be seen in the water. Anacondas quietly wait for animals to come near the water before they attack.

DANGER

People cut down rain forest trees to make room for roads and buildings. They also use the wood to make things like paper and furniture. When several trees get cut down, it is called deforestation.

20

Deforestation destroys many animal homes, which makes it hard for them to survive. When animals find it hard to survive, they are said to be endangered.

ORANGUTANS

As large areas of rain forest are chopped down, orangutans have fewer trees to live and find food in. This can cause orangutans to starve.

22

POISON DART FROGS

Some types of poison dart frogs are endangered. These frogs eat insects on the forest floor, but people are using this space to build farms and buildings.

GLOSSARY

algae   living things that are like plants, but have no roots, stems, leaves or flowers

colony   a nest where ants live together, which is generally underground

endangered   when a species of animal is in danger of going extinct

equator   the imaginary line around Earth that is an equal distance from the North and South Poles

predator   an animal that hunts other animals for food

prey   animals that are hunted by other animals for food

roam   to wander freely or aimlessly, often over a wide area

scale   a small circle of thin bone that protects the skin of fish and reptiles

shelter   protection from danger and harsh weather

starve   when something dies because it doesn't eat enough food

Index

Me vs. Me

Copyright 2019 by Kyeate

Published by Mz. Lady P Presents

All rights reserved

Me vs. Me
Life of Deceit

Kyeate

Connect With Me

Facebook: Author Kyeate/Kyeate Holt

Instagram: Kyewritez

Twitter: adjustnmykrown

Readers, please read before starting:

Before you start this book, this is a rerelease of Charisma vs. Cha Cha, some of my independent work before I signed with Mz. Lady P. This book has been redone and edited. You may have read it, but I recommend reading it again to see changes. Once you finish *Me vs. Me: Life of Deceit* keep turning and read another novella *Deception: City of Lies*, which is also a rerelease. Both books revolve around lies and deceit that causes a blow up of events. Some characters you might be familiar with in some of my other works such as the Miles brothers Darius and Darnell. I hope you enjoy both reads.

~Kyeate

Chapter 1

I harbored so much pain that came from my childhood that it, to an extent, had me heartless. The reason I'm able to recognize it now is because I found someone who cares about me. The demons that sit on my back due to me living a double life was getting heavier. My journey is one that I never prepared for and hoped one day would never catch up with me. My name is Charisma, which is fitting, seeing as though I have the charm to sway a man to do whatever I please. That's my problem though. I seem to use my charm for all the wrong reasons. Most folks call me Cha Cha, which is the part of my life that's conflicting with my future.

"Baby, wake up," the deep raspy sound of the love of my life couldn't sound any better running across my ears.

Kyron was everything, and I loved waking up to him every morning. We had been together for two years. He was the one that as a young girl you would sit up and dream about. He had that thug appeal but respectful man demeanor. Kyron was built like a statue, strong and tall. He had dreads that came to the middle of his back, gray eyes that would cast a spell on you, and he was all mine.

I met Kyron two years ago when he first got out of the penitentiary. Yes, the pen. He did a three-year bid on some drug and gun charges, but he let that life go. He invested his money in some businesses and had been stacking paper the right way ever since. I met him in desperate circumstances. I remember everything as if it happened yesterday.

I had caught a flat in the parking lot where one of his businesses was located and me being the little miss prissy that I am, I had no clue what to do. I was looking around stressed out hoping that someone would offer some assistance.

"It looks to me you need some help, Ms. Lady." His voice instantly made me wet. When I turned to greet the voice, I quickly looked into the eyes of him, my Kyron. Standing up, I adjusted my dress,

"Yes, goodness this damn tire of mine has just been giving me hell," I complained.

"Let me take a look," he suggested. I studied him as he bent down to take a quick look at my tire.

"Do you have a spare in the trunk?" he asked, standing up to look at me. I was so busy looking at his chest and print in his basketball shorts that I had zoned out and didn't hear him.

"Umhm umhm, excuse me? Do you have a spare in your trunk?" he cleared his throat and repeated. I quickly looked up to make eye contact with him, and he was cracking up, showing his beautiful smile.

"What's so funny?" I quizzed. I was embarrassed as hell.

"Yes, I do have a spare in the trunk though," I said quickly popping the trunk and changing the awkwardness in conversation.

He walked around, removed the spare from the trunk, and went to work. The remaining of the time was an awkward silence. About ten minutes later, he was done putting my tire on. Seeing him work and his muscles flex in the sun, and the sweat beads that rolled down his huge arms, made me imagine I was the tire that he was handling.

"This should be good enough for you to drive to the tire shop and get your tire fixed," he said, wiping his hands off on the towel he removed from my trunk. Who the hell told this nigga he could use my good towel?

I shot him a smile, trying not to sound pissed off. "Thank you," I replied.

I think he sensed some sort of attitude from me, so he knocked on my window. Rolling the window down, he handed me a 20-dollar bill.

"Hopefully, this will cover the towel," he said.

"Thank you," I stated, looking away quickly because his eyes were casting a spell on me.

"Why you can't look me in my eyes?" he said smoothly then licked his dark lips.

I started laughing.

"Because those damn gray eyes are hypnotizing, and your smile doesn't make it any better," I admitted. He stooped down so that his face was now in my window.

"Well Ms. Lady, my name is Kyron. Do I have to keep calling you, Ms. Lady?" he asked.

"Not at all, my name is Charisma," I cooed, and from that day forward, we've been together.

I rolled over to greet the voice that I loved to hear so much.

"What baby, why are you waking me up so early?" I pouted as I peeked my head from underneath the covers. Kyron kissed my forehead, something that he always did.

"Well, if you weren't out so late last night, you wouldn't be so tired, and you would realize it's not early, it's one o'clock in the afternoon," he responded.

I rolled over and glanced at the clock and damn it was one something.

"Where did y'all go last night?"

I rose up from the bed quickly to make sure I got my story straight. Even though I had already practiced what I was going to say, I didn't expect him to ask suddenly.

"We really just went bar hopping and to get breakfast," I said scooting out of bed and walking away to the bathroom. Instead of facing the conversation head on, I ran from it.

Starting the shower, I hopped in and took care of my hygiene, making sure that I washed away all of last night's demons. I started to think why in the hell were I still doing the things I did when I had a man that was soon to be my husband. Everything seemed to be going great. I had everything I ever wanted. I owned my own business, car, and all the necessities. My mind started to drift away back to the day that my life was cursed forever.

2011

"You know you're beautiful, and God gave you the body and charm to be able to get what you want in life," said the man.

I was smiling and thinking of all the things I could get that I really needed. Times was hard out here. I was sixteen years old and living with my aunt because my mother had died. I had been living with my aunt all summer, and she was always so damn drunk that she didn't know whether she was coming or going.

"Why are you telling me these things?" I asked laughing at him because I thought it was funny.

"Because you need to know, your auntie ain't gone tell you."

This man called himself schooling me, but for some strange reason, I was checking for him. I was sixteen, and he was twenty-two. I was sitting here smoking weed and hanging out with my auntie's best friend's son. His name was Kasey, but everybody called him Kase. I had been attracted to him for a long time, but of course, he was a grown ass man, and the feeling of my attraction was strange. He always looked at me strangely, but today, maybe it was the weed and being under the influence, I wanted to lose my virginity. I got up to walk in the kitchen to get something to drink when he grabbed me, pulling me back down on the couch onto his lap.

"You ready for school to start back?" he asked me while licking his lips.

"I hate school and auntie talking about me wearing some of her old clothes to school. Who the hell wants to do that?" I complained. That's just how she rocked.

"Shid, I can give you some money to get you some school clothes, but you got to do me a favor," he said with this crazy smirk on his face.

"What's that?" I quizzed, knowing that it had to be some bullshit in the game.

Kase lifted me off his lap, went to the kitchen, and came back with a glass of Kool-Aid, handing it to me. I reached for the glass, and then he handed me a little pill and told me to take it. With no hesitation, I threw the pill back. I already knew it had to be one of the many pills that I see Kase throwback on occasion, so I figured it wouldn't do me any harm.

Kase grabbed me by the hand and led me to my auntie's room. The whole time I was studying him because he wore a grin on his face like he was a kid in the candy store. Even at sixteen, I had curves and ramps as if I had been eating steroid injected chicken since birth. I was giving grown women a run for their money, and I think that's why my aunt acted the way she did towards me. My natural hair came down to the middle of my back. All the guys in the hood were trying to get at me, but of course, I was still a virgin. I knew it had something to do with the girls that I hung around, but I still cherished my innocence— well up until now. Kase laid me on the lumpy bed and unbuckled my pants.

"I'm finna show you how a man is supposed to treat a woman," he whispered in my ear.

My mouth was tight, and I knew he could see my breathing intensified. I felt a throbbing sensation in my coochie that I knew all too well. By that time, I started feeling woozy, and my body had become warm. I felt like I was on top of the world, so I'm pretty sure whatever it was that Kase had given me it was starting to kick in.

Kase removed my panties, and he kissed the inside of my thighs with small kisses leading to my opening. He started moving his tongue in motions. I could tell this was something that he liked to do because he was so into it. He was even moaning and acted as if he was the one being pleasured. Closing my eyes, I laid there and enjoyed the high I was on. I started to tingle inside. I wasn't sure what was happening, but I loved the feeling. It was like a jolt of electricity running through me.

When Kase finally came up for air, he stood up and removed his pants and his boxers. I knew shit was about to get real when he removed his boxers and that thing shot up like a toy popping out of a Jack in the Box.

"Come here let me show you how to please a man," he demanded.

Slowly, I eased up and came face to face with his dick. Never in my life had I had a dick in my face yet along knew what to do with it. Kase gave me instructions telling me to lick it like it was my favorite popsicle. So, I closed my eyes and pretended Kase's dick was a Fudgesicle.

"Damn girl, you sure you ain't done this shit before?" he let out between moans, which made me go even harder. Finally, he told me to stop and climbed on top of me, and he then rammed his dick inside me with so much force.

"Oh my god!" I cried out as I felt a tear roll down the side of my face.

Here I was losing my virginity. The emotions felt good but were so painful. Kase turned into another person while fucking me. I thought my first experience would be nice and gentle, but it was far from it. Kase started to speed up with each stroke and then all of a sudden, I felt him release in me.

Damn, so was this what sex was all about? It felt like we had only been going at it for about fifteen minutes. Kase quickly got up and went in the restroom to clean up. What was I supposed to do? I laid there looking at the ceiling still high off Kase's supply. My insides felt like they had been ripped to shreds. I could hear Kase moving around in the bathroom. At this point, I wanted to roll over and go to sleep. The fire between my legs had me not wanting to move.

The bathroom door flung open, and Kase walked back in fully dressed. Kase tossed a towel at me and told me to clean myself up. Grabbing the towel, I slid off the bed and hurried to the bathroom to clean my lady parts. Letting the warm water soak up the rag I rubbed some soap on it then wiped between my legs. Traces of blood could be seen on the pink towel. Lord, was this supposed to happen. I was freaking out, but I didn't want to say anything to Kase. Pushing my panic thoughts to the back of my head, I continued to clean myself.

When I came back out the restroom, Kase was sitting on the edge of the bed rolling up a blunt. There was an awkward silence in the room between us until Kase stood up to leave.

"I'm only gone tell you this once, keep what happened between us a secret, and keep your fucking legs closed to these niggas out here. I'm the only nigga allowed access to that shit. Do you hear me?" he said rather calmly, pointing to my lower half. I nodded my head yes, he then pulled some money out of his pocket and handed it to me.

"Take this and start looking for you some school clothes," he said, and then he walked out the door as if nothing happened.

As soon as I heard the front door close, I counted the money in my hand. It was $300. I just stood there thinking about what all just happened not knowing that this was the beginning of all Cha Cha's demons.

"Charisma, damn baby, did you get in the tub and drown?" I heard Kyron yell through the door.

I quickly snapped out of my flashback and turned the shower off. Stepping out of the shower, I grabbed my towel hanging on the back of the door and wrapped it around my body. I walked out of the bathroom and Kyron was sitting on the bed.

"My bad baby, that shower was feeling so good," I said as I walked over to him and kissed him on the lips.

"Your phone has been ringing like crazy while you were in the shower," he informed me.

"It probably ain't nobody but Bria or Crystal."

I grabbed the coconut oil from the dresser and began to apply it to my body. I then grabbed my underclothes and threw on my PINK shorts and shirt. Finally, I pulled my hair into a messy bun, threw on some earrings, applied a little lip-gloss, and headed downstairs.

"Where you headed to, baby?" I asked Kyron as he made his way into the kitchen.

"Man, I'm finna head to the shop and see if these niggas got them booth fees and go handle some bills."

He walked by and smacked me on the ass.

"Stop playing, boy!"

"I'm gone get up with you later, what you about to do?" he asked.

"Nothing really other than meet up with Crystal and head to get these nails and feet done."

"Aite when I'm done, I'll hit you up, and we can go eat somewhere later."

"Aite that's fine with me. I love you, baby!"

"I love you too, girl," he said as he walked out the door.

As soon as Kyron walked out the door, I looked at my iPhone and saw I had five missed calls and three text messages. *Damn, who in the hell been blowing me up? Ugh, what the hell does Taye want?* I pressed his number to call him back.

"Aye, girl!" the voice on the other end of the phone said.

"Nigga why in the fuck you blowing me up like this and you know I'm at home with my nigga!" I yelled into the phone.

"Man, chill the fuck out Cha Cha. I can't find my fucking wallet. Can you look in your car under the seat or something?" Taye asked.

Fucking dumb ass.

"Ugh, man hold on. I'm on my way out to the car now," I hissed.

Walking out to the car I unlocked the door and started looking around the car, and sho nuff his wallet was laying in the floorboard of my car. Good thing Kyron took his truck to work and not my car because some days he would randomly switch up.

"Yeah, it's in here. Where you at?" I sighed.

"I'm headed to the house. Meet me there," he said and hung up the phone.

Rude ass bitch, he had better be glad that his dick game was proper and he keeps my pockets fat because otherwise, I would let him have it.

Chapter 2

You're probably wondering who the hell Taye is, right. He's just another bad habit that I couldn't seem to break. I met him two months ago and had been milking his pockets ever since. Last night I told Kyron that I went out with my homegirls, which I really did, but I left with Taye. My problem is I don't really understand why I sleep with other men while I'm with Kyron, who caters to my every need and treats me like a queen. It's like it fills a void in me or gives me the security for my fear of being alone. In the back of my mind, I have this fear that Kyron is too good for me and he will leave, so if he ever does, I'll have a backup plan.

I pulled up to his condo in Germantown, hopped out of my Camaro, and walked to his unit. Before I even got a chance to knock on the door, Taye opened the door.

"Here boy!" I yelled as I threw his wallet in his hands and walked past him.

"Damn, well hi to you too, Cha Cha." Taye closed the door, and I walked over and took a seat on the couch.

"Man, I was looking all over for this damn thing." He walked over and kissed me on the cheek.

I didn't take my eyes off him because I felt a certain way. It was like something was up, and I didn't like that feeling. Taye was easy on the eyes, but he wasn't the finest thing. His money was long, and that helped me stick around.

"You look nice today, bae," he complimented me.

"Thank you, Taye," I answered rudely.

He had me irritated as the fuck with him for the simple fact this nigga was slipping big time. Taye had mentioned plenty times that whenever he finds out who my nigga was, he was gone make it his duty to break up our relationship because he was tired of sharing. He was on bitch nigga shit. See, that's the only problem about messing with these niggas. They end up catching feelings and shit and just weren't satisfied for shit. This was my cue to leave this nigga now before things got out of hand.

"Look Taye. I can't do this anymore," I blurted out as I turned to look him in his eyes. "I really just need some time to get things together and determine what it is I want. I just need to focus on myself right now."

"You're trying to cut me off, huh? That means you must be finna cut your nigga off too, right?" he asked. I looked around to see who this nigga was talking to.

"No, I've been with him for two years, I'm not about to end what we have, I know for a fact that what he and I have is real and what we been doing was just fun."

Taye got up and paced the floor talking to himself. I knew he was mad because that's what he did every time he got mad.

"You know what, Cha Cha. You're a fucking joke. You've probably been cheating on this nigga the whole time you been with him, and you're trying to play me right now. I knew I should've listened to your girl Bria when she said you were a hoe!" he spat.

"Hold up, what the fuck you mean you should've listened to Bria, What the fuck y'all doing discussing me?" I asked, getting up off the couch and up in his face.

He chuckled a little too much for my liking, so I hauled off and smacked the shit out of him. Taye grabbed his face and bit his lip. I wanted this nigga to jump stupid.

"You know what Taye, fuck you!" I said as I turned and walked off. Taye followed me out of the door trying to argue and shit, but I wasn't trying to hear shit he had to say.

"Cha Cha, you dead ass right now?" I could feel him walking up behind me, so I quickly turned around.

"Look Taye. I'm gone advise you to back the fuck away from me, before I let off these rounds in your motherfucking ass," I threatened. I was licensed to carry, and I didn't mind letting loose if I had to. Taye stopped in his tracks and watched me get in the car and pull off.

Once I started driving, I started to think to myself this bitch Bria got another thing coming. I couldn't believe that Bria had been fucking Taye behind my back, but at the same time, I wouldn't put it past that bitch. Maybe this was a sign that I needed to quit doing what all I had been doing.

Needing to clear my mind, I just drove and drove until I ended up in LaVergne. I ended up pulling up in front of the house that I wasn't a stranger to. I really don't know what lead me here. Maybe it was to confront my demons. At this point, my mind drifted away thinking back to how things with Kase and me went from sweet to sour all too fast.

It seems like the day after Kase took my virginity he took control of my mind and my heart. I would do anything for him, no questions asked, and he would do the same for me in return. Things between Kase and I had gotten to the point where all our sneaking around had finally caught up with us. One Friday night he had come and picked me up from my auntie's so that we could go hang out and get something to eat. As soon as I hopped in the truck, he passed me the blunt. I took a couple of hits and started to feel good.

"I needed that baby," I whispered as I laid my head back on the headrest. I was stressed out, and I knew it was wearing me down.

"Why you sound like you had a stressful day, girl?" he asked, sounding concerned.

"That's because I did. I haven't been feeling too well."

"Well, we finna hit this party at my homeboy's crib, so shit, you'll be aite in no time," Kase said. We continued to pass the blunt around and carrying on conversation.

When we pulled up in front of Kase's homeboy house and got out of the car. I knew it was finna be a house full of niggas just by all the cars that were in the yard. Kase walked me in the house and just as

I thought, it was a house full of niggas. This was some shit that I wouldn't dare step in alone. I was the only girl. I turned to Kase.

"What kind of party is this, and why am I the only girl?" I whispered.

"Quit tripping. You're my little lady. Ain't nothing finna happen to you, you'll be aite," he reassured me.

"What up, Kase?" hollered one of the guys whom I recognized because I had seen him before. Kase walked over to the guy and gave him a pound on the hand.

"What up, my nigga?"

"Excuse me guys, I have to go to ladies' room," I said, walking off feeling uncomfortable because all eyes were on me.

The funny thing though even being her with Kase, I felt uncomfortable, and I couldn't shake the nervous feeling that I had in the pit of my stomach. When I entered the bathroom, I sat down on the toilet seat trying to get my head together. This nigga is talking about he wants to spend time with me, yet he brings me over here to a goddamn house full of niggas. Ugh, my nerves were irked to the fucking max. After a few moments with my thoughts, I stood up and looked in the mirror at myself, fixed my shirt, and applied some lip-gloss before walking back out to the living room.

When I walked out of the door, Kase was standing there waiting on me, scaring the fuck out of me. I jumped so fast.

"Cha Cha, let me holler at you for a second," he said, pulling me to the side.

"You know how you are always saying you would do anything for me because you love me, right?" I nodded my head not sure where this was going.

"Well, I need you to do me a huge favor. I need you to make my nigga in there happy. He just broke up with his gal, and he's all depressed and shit."

"What that got to do with me, how do you expect me to make him happy. What exactly are you saying, Kase?" My voice was trembling because I knew he wasn't asking what I think he was asking.

"You need to use what I taught you and work that charm of yours," he said.

At that time, I saw something in Kase's eyes that I had never seen. It was like he was possessed. I was shocked at the fact that he asked me because he always was so adamant with me about fucking other guys. However, I figured since he was setting it up for his boy that it wouldn't be a problem. I told him ok that I would do it, but I wasn't happy, and the only reason that I was doing this was because he asked me to.

Kase clinched his jaws and walked off. I followed him into the living room, and he told me to go upstairs. With fear in my body, I started to walk upstairs, and when I turned to look at Kase, he shook his head as if he was mad at me. Quickly turning his head, he started talking to his nigga. At that moment I was confused as to why in the hell was Kase acting so angry when this was his doing.

Walking down the hall, I entered the first bedroom I saw, closing the door behind me. I was really hoping tonight would've gone differently. I was hoping to tell Kase that I missed my period and I think I might be pregnant. I had to tell him soon. That's when my phone started vibrating, and it was a text from Kase.

Kasey: MY NIGGA SAID MAKE SURE ALL THE LIGHTS ARE TURNED OFF!

I wanted to cry and run out of here so bad. Placing my phone back in my purse, I got up and cut the lights off. About five minutes later, I heard a knock on the door. No response or movement came from me, but I listened as the guy made his way into the room and closer to the bed. It was so dark in the damn room that I couldn't see shit. That's when I felt a gentle caress on my face. Closing my eyes, I envisioned Kase rubbing my face. Then I heard him unzip his pants. The gentleness had gone out the window, and my head was grabbed with so much force and pushed towards the guy's dick. I didn't want to do this, but I closed my eyes, imagined that it was Kase, and went to work. By the faint moans that came from him, I knew I was handling my business. In a swift motion, he forcefully pulled my pants down and got on top of me.

"You're hurting me," I cried out. That's when he placed his hands over my mouth.

"You're just a fucking little hoe. I told your ass to never let another nigga in between your legs and what do you do the first chance you get? You do it," the familiar voice said catching me off guard.

"Wait a minute, Kase?" I yelled out.

SMACK! SMACK!

My face was stinging from the two smacks that landed on my face. Grabbing my face, I started to cry harder. When I looked up the lights was on, and Kase was standing there looking at me like he was about to kill me.

"You failed, Cha Cha!" he barked.

"I trusted you to do the right thing, and you were sitting here letting me do all those things to you. Good thing it was me and not my nigga," he continued.

"Kase, I only did it because you asked me to, I would never intentionally fuck another nigga. Why would you do this me and then try to turn it on me? You came to me. What was I supposed to do?" I cried.

"Maybe stood up to me like a woman would have and told me to go to hell, and how you weren't finna fuck nobody. Damn, I thought I taught you better, but you still a little bitty ass girl." He paced the floor, shaking his head.

"I think we need some time apart. Get your shit on so that I can take you home," he said as he turned and walked out the room.

I stood up putting my pants back on while the tears burned my eyes. What in the fuck happened and what was the point? The shit he did was foul and wasn't cool at all. I walked back downstairs, and everybody was looking at me shaking they head. I just held my head down and walked out of the house.

***

The ride home was so damn silent that it scared me. I needed to break the silence, but I wasn't sure how until I saw the Walgreens sign down the street.

"Kase, can please you stop at the Walgreens before you drop me off?" I asked. Kase looked at me disgusted

"What you need from there that can't wait?" I looked at him like he was crazy

"A pregnancy test!" I shouted

"What? Wait a minute, a what? A pregnancy test! When the fuck was you gone say something to me about this?"

"First off, stop yelling at me! I thought we were going to dinner or something tonight and I was gone tell you then. Didn't you hear me say that I wasn't feeling well? Nah, you probably didn't because your motherfucking ass was so wrapped up in this funky ass set up that you had planned, you weren't paying attention," I fumed. He looked at me like I was crazy.

"Yeah motherfucker, you done pissed me off. Remember all that you taught me. You not finna talk to me like I'm some random ass

hoe. Yeah true enough I was finna fuck your friend, but I was fucking you. You should've sent your nigga upstairs for real if you really wanted to test me. Then you would've really been pissed because this charm I got, that you showed me how to use, I would've had your nigga coming up out his pockets with enough money to break me and you both off. Now can you please pull over so that I can get a damn test," I said and rolled my eyes and looked out the window.

Kase pulled over to the Walgreens and put the car in park. He reached in his pocket to hand me a twenty.

"I don't need your fucking money!" I spat as I got out and slammed the door.

For some reason I was feeling fucking good, I had never in my life spoke to anyone like that, not even Kase. I went inside the store and purchased the pregnancy test.

***

Sitting here looking at both tests I took I couldn't believe I was pregnant. Well actually, I could because Kase never used a condom with me. This would be Kase first child, but I wasn't ready for no damn baby. Trying to weigh my options and my future, I was clueless on what to do.

Chapter 3

Sitting here in front of this house, I really couldn't believe I drove here. I had so many damn demons, and this was the biggest damn one I had hiding. I eased out of the car and walked up to the door and rang the doorbell.

"Who is it?" I heard the familiar voice say.

"Charisma!" I said loud enough to be heard. The door opened, and there was my baby daddy Kase. For thirty years old, he still looked twenty-two and was still as sexy as ever.

"Cha Cha, what are you doing here?" he said with a grin on his face.

"Well, can I come in or I got to stand on the porch?" I asked. He stood to the side and let me in. Looking around, taking in my surroundings, I turned to face him.

"Actually, I was just thinking and driving, and I ended up here," I admitted.

Kase walked over to me and hugged me. Being in his arms felt good for right now. He was my security. We stood and hugged for what seems like forever. It always felt good to be in Kase's arms.

"Who was at the door, daddy?" I heard the little voice say. I turned around to welcome it.

"Mommy!" my son yelled out in excitement as he ran and gave me a big hug.

situated and tucked him in. Leaving was the hardest part every time. The shit never got easy.

"Well Kase I'm finna head back down this road, I'll talk to y'all later," I quickly said as I hurried out the door. If I had of stayed any longer Kase would've continued to try his hand.

***

Kyron was blowing up my phone, so I knew I was late. Powering off my phone came to mind so that I could use my battery is dead line. I was doing eighty in a sixty fuck a ticket in my Camaro down that highway like I was running from the police. Me telling Kase that I wasn't fucking around anymore I meant that not just with him, but I was done with the random niggas. Change had to start somewhere.

Hitting my exit, I stopped at Exxon to get me some cigars. Putting the car in park, I exited quick as hell because I already was behind. I hopped out of the car dropping my keys. When I bent over to get my keys, I heard a male voice say

"You shouldn't bend over like that with all that hanging out them shorts," the guy said.

I picked my keys up and looked back at this nigga walking towards me. Not even paying attention, I laughed and continued my walk into the store.

"Can I get a pack of White Owls?" I asked the store clerk.

Removing five dollars from my wallet, I gave the clerk the money and got my change. When I turned to walk out the store, I couldn't help but notice that the guy that had spoken to me outside was sexy as fuck. It was time for me to put my charm to work, so I walked up to him

"Did you call yourself flirting with me?" I asked.

He quickly turned around with a smile on his face smiling showing me those pearly white teeth. He looked like a decadent chocolate bar. I took a quick glance at his ensemble a pair of Balmain jeans, Louboutin sneakers, and a white shirt, but his jewelry topped it off. *This nigga look and smell like money.*

"I mean I wasn't necessarily flirting, but I couldn't help but look," he said. I extended my hand.

"Cha Cha is my name. Can I have the honor of knowing yours?" I flirted, laying it on thick. He reached out and shook my hand

"Cha Cha, I know that can't be your real name. My name is Cam."

"Well Cam, I'm in a rush right now and your right my real name isn't Cha Cha, but I'm going to give you my number, and you can hit me up sometime this week, and we can do lunch and get to know each other a little better. Is that ok with you?" I suggested.

"Yeah I can dig it."

Cam handed me his phone, and I placed my number inside. I hit him with a wink and walked on out of the store. Once I got in the car, I decided to sit there and see what kind of car he got in. A couple of minutes later, Cam exited the store and hopped in an all-black matte Jeep Wrangler with black rims. *Jackpot*! I thought as I smiled and pulled off.

***

When I finally arrived home, I noticed Kyron's car sitting in the driveway, and the house was pretty dark. *This nigga is probably in here sleep.* I got out of the car and made my way into the house. One thing I hated was walking into a dark house. Kyron knew I hated that shit. I headed upstairs to the bedroom we shared. When I walked into the room, I wasn't ready for the surprise that awaited me. There were candles lit going in a trail leading to the bathroom. *What the fuck this nigga got going on? It bet not be no bitch up in my motherfucking house.*

Entering the bathroom, the bubble bath with rose petals, two wine glasses, and a bottle of Moët sitting next to the tub caught my attention. When I turned around to walk out, there stood Kyron, looking sexy as ever in his polo boxers, and he had his dreads freshly twisted. I made a mental note to ask his ass about that later because don't nobody does his hair but me.

"Hey, baby. I figured by time you got here you wouldn't want to go out, so I decided to be a little romantic and planned this. By the way, I tried calling your phone."

"Yeah, I'm sorry about that, baby. My damn phone went dead," I lied showing him my phone. This man always did what he could to keep me happy, and this was why I knew I had to stop hoeing around. I couldn't risk losing him.

"This looks nice, baby. What did I do to deserve all this?" I asked while I started removing my clothes so that I can get in the tub.

"Baby, every now and then we both are so busy and wrapped up in our lives that we never really have time for just us, so I figured a little surprise wouldn't hurt," he answered.

I stepped in the tub and Kyron poured me a glass of Moët.

"Here you go. Just relax, and I'm going downstairs and take care of something."

"Ok, baby," I said as I grabbed the glass and took a sip.

While I sat in the tub sipping on my drink getting a little buzz, I laid my head back, closed my eyes, and just started to think back on some things. After I had KJ, Kase, and I really didn't do the relationship thing. Now don't get me wrong. He was my baby daddy, so we still fucked, and of course, he still tried to control my pussy. That's when I started going beast mode on niggas. See, Kase fucked me up in the head. Yeah, he taught me some things, but I was very bitter after that bullshit ass test he pulled on me. I was only sixteen. I loved Kase, but he couldn't see that. It's funny he tries to see that shit now, but hell it's too late.

All through high school, I wouldn't dare date the high school boys. They didn't have enough money for me, so I started messing around with the little dope boys that had a little change. On the weekends, I would go to Clarksville with Bria and Crystal, so hell, I started fucking around with them city niggas and taking they money. You're probably calling me a little hoe, but at some point, I liked these niggas.

Now at the age of twenty-four, every time I try to stop, I fall weak to some handsome ass nigga. I kind of told Kyron what I wanted him to know about my promiscuous past. I just kept the fact that I have a seven-year-old son and that I'm currently sleeping around on him a secret. This man asks me all the time when we can start a family, and I just keep throwing up a million excuses. The battle I fight with myself is killing me. Charisma is who I'm trying to be, which is who Kyron sees, and Cha Cha is that bitch just about her paper and has no remorse for what she does. Something got to give before Cha Cha is the death of Charisma.

The water had gotten cold, so I got up to get out the tub. Grabbing the towel that Kyron had laid out, I walked into the bedroom and saw that he had laid out a little something he wanted me to put on. So, I oiled up my body, and I put on the baby doll chemise he had purchased from Victoria Secret. I threw on my slipper heels and walked downstairs. I followed the rose petals, which led me to our backyard. Kyron was sitting in the gazebo on pillows when I walked up to him. Looking around at the setup, I noticed he had my favorite foods and dessert sitting out picnic style.

"Oh my god baby, this is so freaking romantic. I think I'm gone cry."

"Oh no, you're not. No crying, not even happy tears," he smiled.

I sat down, we ate dinner, and we started talking and laughing about things that we did when we first met. The mood was great, and I didn't want to kill it, but I had to know about his hair.

"I noticed you got your hair re-twisted. When did you start letting other folks do your hair?" I asked with a lifted brow.

"I figured you wouldn't have time to do it, so Bria came over here and did it," he calmly said. My head whipped up fast as hell.

"Bria, what the fuck!" I said, snapping.

"Yeah baby, what's the problem? Hell, she's your friend?" he shrugged.

I needed to bring it down a few notches. I quickly remembered that he doesn't know I want to bust Bria's shit wide the fuck open, so I had to flip it.

"I just don't like other people touching your hair."

"Well baby, I promise won't nobody else touch my hair," he smiled. He crawled over to where I was laying and kissed my forehead.

That night Kyron and I made passionate love almost half the night outside in the gazebo, and then we finished in the bedroom until the sun rose.

Chapter 4

The next morning my alarm went off about eleven a.m. I had a client at noon, so I dragged my ass out of bed and went to the bathroom to brush my teeth and shower. One thing about me, I had my own money, but I loved spending others. I owned my own beauty salon. Doing hair was something that I always wanted to do. When I came out, Kyron was still sleeping. He had put in work last night, so he was going to be out for a minute.

I walked over to my closet, pulled out some black Nike yoga leggings and a Nike top, and threw on a pair of Air Max. Looking into the mirror, I thought about how I was about to do my hair. I hated my hair. It was so damn unmanageable at times, and I hated combing it. I just let it all hang down today in its natural state. Before I left out for the day, I walked over to Kyron kissing him and letting him know that I was headed to work.

When I arrived at the shop my best friend, Crystal was there and was already working on her client.

"Hey, girl!" I greeted her as I walked past her to my station

"Hey, lady!"

"Girl, I got some shit to tell you about your friend Bria. That trick got it coming."

"Damn, what the hell I miss?" Crystal laughed.

I gave her a look letting her know that I would fill her in when we were alone. I got settled in and started on my client. About an hour into my work, my cell started ringing. I didn't recognize the number, so finally, I answered.

"Hello!"

"Hey, big booty," the voice on the other end said, and I started laughing. I knew then it wasn't nobody but Cam.

"Cam, is that how you talk on the phone?" I asked.

"I can talk a little nastier, but it's not the time for all that right now. Anyway, what are you up to?" he asked.

"Right now, I'm working on my client."

"Ah, so you do hair, huh? What time do you think you'll be done? I'm trying to see you today," he voiced.

"This is my only client for the day, so I'll hit you up soon as I get done."

"That's what's up, Cha Cha, I'll be waiting," he said and hung up the phone. I was kind of excited about meeting up with Cam. Something about him seemed to move me. Who am I kidding? Maybe it was just the money?

I finally finished up with my client and went back to my office to finish some paperwork. Crystal walked in and sat down across from me. Crystal had been my girl since I moved in with my auntie when I was sixteen. She lived across the street from me. Now, Bria, I met a little after high school right before cosmetology school. She was one of them friends that you always questioned they behavior. I sholl in the hell did from time to time. She had this sneakiness to her that I vowed to always watch, and now that Taye told me they fucked, and I heard she did Kyron's hair, I knew the bitch had motives.

"So girl what's the tea with Miss Bria? Crystal asked.

"Let me tell you about this bitch. So, you know the other night I left the club with Taye, right. Why does he call me the next day looking for his wallet? Girl, when I found the shit, I took it to him. I got there, and for some reason, my conscious kicked in. I got the feeling bad, so I told him I wasn't really feeling our little situation anymore. Long story short, Taye and I got into a heated argument, and he tells me he fucked Bria," I said.

"Bitch, you lying!" Crystal interrupted.

"Bitch, if I'm lying, I'm flying. But wait, to make matters worse, Kyron let this bitch in my house yesterday to do his hair."

"Hold up. Kyron doesn't let anybody touch his hair. Hell, I'm cold with the dreads, and he came by the shop yesterday looking for you to do his shit. I offered, and he said no, but he let Bria do it?" she said while shaking her head.

"See, I didn't know he came by here, and you offered. Something ain't right about that bullshit," I said, scratching my head.

I sat there quietly because I was really thinking about what the fuck was going on. Would Kyron ever cheat on me was the question? I already knew Bria's intentions, but if this was my karma, I was prepared to go to war.

"Where were you at yesterday anyway, honey?" Crystal asked.

"I went to LaVergne and seen KJ," I said.

"Oh, how's he doing?"

"He's doing good. His daddy ass is still trying to get with me, but I ain't having that," I said. My cell phone started ringing. It was Kyron

"Hey baby," I answered.

"Wassup with you?" he replied.

"Nothing much, I'm good, just sitting here in the office talking to Crystal, I didn't know you came by the shop yesterday, and she offered to do your hair," I said sarcastically. "You seem to leave that little detail out yesterday."

"Baby, are you trying to get around to something? Stop with all the beating around the bush shit," Kyron said rudely. It took me by surprise.

"You goddamn right I'm trying to say something. Stay the fuck away from that conniving little bitch Bria!" I yelled.

"Charisma, do you hear yourself right now? You sound like a mad woman. I ain't stuttin' Bria's nasty ass. She done fucked half my crew, so whatever she got up her sleeve or dress, I ain't falling for that shit. I only let her do my hair because she came by the house to drop

Loco off, and I didn't want Crystal knowing my surprise because she would've told you," he said.

Damn, I didn't know Bria was slutting it up like that. That girl tries so hard to be like me it's sick. Now that's the one thing I wouldn't do, fuck somebody that Kyron knows or associates himself with in any way. I guess maybe I was tripping, but I still got to confront this bitch, because she's barking up the wrong tree.

"Anyway, I was calling to let you know I'm about to hook up with my nigga from Atlanta and we finna discuss another business venture," Kyron said.

"Ok, that's fine. I'm finna go work out with Crystal anyway. I love you, and I'll talk to you later, baby," I said and ended our conversation.

Little did Kyron know I had a little business to tend to of my own, I quickly dialed Cam's number, and he picked up on the first ring

"Sup, Ms. Cha Cha, what do I owe this pleasure?" he asked.

"I was just calling to ask could I take a rain check. My girlfriend and I have some business we need to tend to."

"Oh, so you don't have a nigga, you like girls?" he asked jokingly.

"Excuse me, no fool. I like dick only. Do not fade me like that."

"Baby, I'm just fucking with you but yeah that's cool I got something important that I got to handle anyway, and I didn't know how long it was gone last," he said.

"Well, I'll be sure to hit you up later on then."

"Aite boo," he replied, and we hung up the phone.

I texted Bria asking her to meet Crystal and me at the park so that we can work out, and she was with it.

Looking over at Crystal, I voiced. "You ready to go handle this wax?" I asked.

"What wax? What you done got me into now? You already know I'm riding off the top." she asked even though I knew she was down before asking.

"We finna meet Bria at the park to workout that's all," I answered with an evil grin.

"Workout, really Charisma? Is that what you call an ass whooping these days?" She laughed. I burst out laughing myself. But hell, this was liable to be a workout because when we fought, we fought dirty, and Bria did too.

We closed up shop and cleaned up. We then hopped in my car and headed to Hartman Park. I knew my ass was too old to be out here fighting, but this was about my respect. Bria was moving grimy as hell. As we neared the park, I noticed Bria's car sitting in the lot, so I pulled in right beside her. She was on the phone, gums flapping as usual. Once she noticed it was me beside her, she rolled the window down and so did I

"Hey, chicas!" she said all excited. I played it off.

"Hey, girl!" I said.

"Hold on let me finish this call," she yelled.

I rolled the window back up and turned to look at Crystal, shaking my head. That bitch disgusts me. It was a hot ass day, and the guys were on the court, shirts off, basketball shorts hanging with sweat glistening off all the different shades of chocolate. As I continued to gawk, my eyes ran over a very familiar body. It was none other than Taye's funky ass looking dead at me like he saw a damn ghost. Well, he was in for a show today.

"Look at this shit," I told Crystal, pointing to Taye.

"Umhmm," was all she said.

Crystal and I hopped out the car and headed over to one of the benches. I pulled my hair up into a knotted bun on top of my head since bitches love grabbing hair. The tension in the air was as thick as the damn humidity. When I turned, Taye's ass was staring a hole in me, but I didn't even acknowledge him.

"Sup hoes, y'all ready?" Bria said as she made her way over to us. Crystal and I both said yes in unison. So, we all started stretching and laughing and talking like ain't shit happened.

"Bria, you did Kyron's hair yesterday?" I threw out there.

"Um yeah, he couldn't find nobody to do it, so I handled it for him," she answered as she switched arms in between stretching.

"Girl, why does Taye ass keep looking over here? I bet he scared trying to figure out what we are talking about." Crystal laughed.

"He did enough talking for all three of us yesterday," I said.

"Did I miss something? Ooh, catch me up. What's the tea with you and Taye?" she asked. I looked over at Crystal then I stopped walking and turned to Bria.

"How about I tell you what you missed. The fact that you been fucking Taye behind my back and that I know what you trying to do to Kyron!" I snapped. With my arms crossed and waiting to hear what the hell she had to say, this hoe just bust out laughing.

"See Cha Cha. You don't even get it, do you? You think you can run around here just doing your dirt and nobody gets hurt. Yeah, you right I fucked Taye. I figured you really liked him, but he was just too easy to give up the dick. I like a challenge, and I know Kyron would be the perfect challenge," she taunted.

"Really bitch!" yelled Crystal.

"It's ok, Crystal. This bitch is delusional that's all. First off, I could care less about Taye. You didn't hurt my pockets. Yeah, you might have fucked him, but I bet you he didn't come out his pockets not once for your dusty, broke down, stretched out pussy ass. Now Kyron, he got standards boo, and from what I heard, you're fucking the crew, so you wouldn't have gotten far with him. But I will tell you this, if you think for one second you gone run your mouth to Kyron about what I'm doing, you better think again!" I spat, getting in her face.

"What exactly are you gone do, Cha Cha?" she said, poking me in the chest with her finger.

No, this bitch didn't!

Reflex mode kicked in, and I grabbed her finger and bent that shit all the way back while she screamed out in pain.

"Bitch, I will erase you like I drew you!" I spat.

Bria was still screaming out in pain because I had broken her finger. She used her other hand to swing at me. That's when I threw her ass on the ground and started punching her in the face. By that time, a crowd had started to form, and Bria ass was a lost cause. I got up off her ass and turned to walk away, and she hopped up and came charging at me. I heard Taye say Cha Cha, and I turned around, and Crystal had rocked Bria ass to sleep with a one-hitter quitter. I walked over to Bria and got down close enough and lifted her head by grabbing her hair and I whispered to her.

"Bitch, you know I got peoples, and all I got to do is say the word, and your ass would come up missing. I advise you to act like you don't know me or leave this motherfucking state," I said, slamming her head back down on the concrete. I walked off to my car and Taye ran up beside me

"You ok, Cha Cha?" he had the nerve to ask.

"I'm fine. Go check on your bitch," I said, and Crystal and I pulled off.

Chapter 5
Kyron

A nigga had just pulled up at Donk's Bar and Grill to meet with my boy for this business meeting. Today had gone well, and this was finna top it off. I hopped out of the car and made my way into the bar.

"Welcome to Donks!" the waitresses said in unison.

Hitting them with a head nod and a smile, I noticed my boy sitting in the back. I headed over to his table

"What up witcha, nigga?" I greeted him, giving my nigga dap.

"Man nothing much, enjoying this damn view. The ladies in here are bad as hell."

"Yeah they are. I try to stay out of here as much as possible. My gal would kill me if she knew I was lusting to smack one of these asses in here," I admitted, and we both laughed.

"So what's up you thinking about moving up here permanently?" I asked.

"Nah, I may be making it my second home, but you know I ain't leaving Atlanta."

"All well that's what's up, so let's talk business then, my nigga."

My nigga and I sat there and talked for damn near two hours. We lost track of time and had drunk a whole damn bottle of 1800. I was huge on energy, and the energy was good, and we were vibing. My phone started to ring, and I looked at the caller ID seen it was my boy Roy calling.

"What's up, Roy?" I spoke into the phone.

"Man, have you talked to your gal?"

"No why, what's up? Is she aite?" I asked nervously.

"Oh, I'm sure she aite, but Bria not. Charisma beat the brakes off Bria at the park today," he said.

"What! Nigga, you lying?" I replied

"Bruh, I'm dead ass serious. Call her and ask her yourself."

"Man, aite nigga," I said and hung up.

"Everything aite?" my nigga asked.

"Yeah man. My gal done beat the fuck out of one of her friends at the park today." I sighed and shook my head. This bet not be about the conversation we had today. Me and my nigga started laughing.

"Let me call her and see what the fuck is up," I said, and I dialed Charisma's number.

"Hello?" Charisma answered the phone.

"You got something you need to tell me?" I asked. She started laughing

"You sound more like my daddy than my nigga, but for your information, I guess me telling you that I beat the hell out of Bria is what you referring to. I beat that hoe ass and told her to get ghost before I make her disappear," she said so calmly that shit scared me.

"Charisma, please tell me you didn't beat her ass because she did my hair?" I asked.

"Hell no, that shit was deeper. She had been doing some foul shit then when I confronted her, she went all Billy Badass on me and tried telling me about myself and then admitted to trying to seduce you. That hoe put her hands on me and ask what I was gone do. Now why in the hell did she do that? Baby, I broke that bitch's finger."

"Girl, you crazy as fuck. Man, I'll be home in a minute girl. I love you," I said.

"I love you too, Kyron!"

I hung up the phone and shook my head because that shit was crazy and wild that she was out here showing her ass like that. Charisma was hood as hell.

"Man, my gal is crazy as hell. She done beat gal ass, broke her finger, and then told her to leave town before she disappears," I said to my nigga.

"Damn, remind me not to get on her bad side," my nigga joked.

"Let me get up out of here and head to the house. This 1800 got me feeling good, and I'm finna bust some moves on my baby when I get home. All this ass up in here got me feeling some type of way," I admitted.

"Aite then nigga, shit I'm finna hit up this shorty I met last night and see what she's talking about, ya feel me?" he said.

"Yeah, I feel you, my nigga, hit me up tomorrow sometime. We can go look at the site where you want to open up shop."

"Aite Kyron, good looking out."

"No problem, Cam," I said and walked out.

Chapter 6
Charisma

I wasn't sure if Bria was gone keep my secret, but honestly, if she knew what was good for her, she would. She knew I had connections, and I'll have her ass floating in the Cumberland River somewhere. Every time I saw her, I was gone beat that ass till she got the picture. Since I made it home, I had showered and dressed down comfortable while curled up on the couch watching *Love & Hip-Hop Atlanta* and my phone started ringing. It was Cam.

"Hey, Cam."

"Sup with you my girl what you up to?" he asked.

"Nothing much just sitting her watching TV. What you up to?" I asked while twirling my hair.

"Man, I'm finna head back to the room. I done had a little too much to drink. I think you should come and visit me," he said.

"Your room, you not from here?" I asked curiously.

"I guess since we ain't met up yet to have our getting to know each other session you wouldn't know. But nah shawty, I'm from Atlanta. I'm getting a place here though because I'm opening a business here with my homeboy. How about you let me come through, and we can talk about all we need to talk about?" he said.

"Well, since we're sort of telling each other little things about each other, I guess I should tell you that I have a man," I admitted.

"What's that supposed to mean? We're grown. We can do us without getting caught."

"Yeah true, but not tonight. Hey, I got to go. My boyfriend is here. I'll talk to you soon," I said quickly and hung up the phone when I heard the keys jiggling in the door.

I tossed the phone and closed my eyes pretending to be sleep when I heard Kyron walking towards the living room. He walked in the room and kneeled in my face, I knew because of the pungent smell of liquor I could smell on his breath.

"Well, I know what you been drinking on tonight. Where have you been? Let me guess, Donks?" I mumbled, opening my eyes. Kyron grinned with his eyes half closed.

This nigga was drunk as hell.

"Yes mama, I had a little too much 1800. So now you got to tend to daddy." He licked his lips.

"Kyron, you need to go sleep that off. Nah, you need to go shower, smelling like a big ass bottle and weed. You not finna get in my bed like that!" I yelled because I was a tad bit irritated. I really hate when Kyron drank too much. He could get really worrisome.

"Come on. You finna take a shower," I said hopping up off the couch and grabbing his hand leading him to the bathroom.

Kyron propped himself up on the bathroom wall as I started the shower for him and helped him get undressed. Goodness, his body was turning me on just looking at him. I just stood there looking at this tatted muscular machine as he climbed in the shower.

While he was in the shower, I had climbed in bed and was laying there. I was tired as hell, so for a moment there I had dozed off. When I felt a wetness between my legs, I tried moving my legs, but Kyron had a grip on them and wasn't letting go. This man was handling his business. The way the warmth of his tongue felt sliding across my clit, sent chills through my body. Kyron could eat the fuck out of some pussy.

My hands wrapped around his dreads, and he wrote a cursive love poem on my clit. The feeling was euphoric. I felt I was about to reach my peak, and my legs started quivering. Kyron brought his face to meet mine. We held each other's gaze for what felt like forever, and then he slowly entered me. Something about the sex tonight felt strange. Don't get me wrong it was amazing. It was just a bad feeling I had.

***

The next morning, I had woken up rather early because I couldn't sleep. I had been tossing and turning most of the night. Kyron must have had a busy day because he was already gone. Sitting on the side of the bed, I decided to call Cam. I knew he probably would have a hangover from being fucked up last night. The phone rang about three times, and with no answer, I decided to hang up. No sooner than I hung up the phone, it rang back. Cam was calling back.

"I thought you were asleep. I wasn't trying to wake you," I said.

"Girl, money never sleeps. I've been up and out. I had to meet my homeboy and go look at this property, and then I went and put a down payment on me a condo," he informed me.

"So, you've pretty much been busy. I was gone to see if you wanted to hang today. That's if you can."

"Of course, have you eaten breakfast yet?"

"No, I literally just got up."

"How about we meet at The Pancake Pantry?" he suggested.

"That's fine with me. Give me about forty-five minutes," I told him.

"Ok that's cool," he said.

After we hung up the phone, I got up to run and take a quick shower. I was excited to meet up with Cam. I know I said I was done playing around, but the thrill and getting to know what he was about made it to where I just couldn't help myself. When I got done taking my shower, I oiled my body in coconut oil. Good thing I had rolled my hair the night before, so I threw on my cute little sundress, my wedges and applied a little bit of makeup. After a quick once-over and being satisfied with how I came together, I left the house on cloud nine.

The Pancake Pantry was a fifteen-minute drive from where I lived. On the drive over, I placed my phone on silent. When I pulled up, I spotted Cam's Jeep parked near the entrance. Looking in the mirror, I checked my face and teeth making sure I was presentable before I stepped out the vehicle. When I walked up to the door, Cam greeted me with a hug and a quick peck on the cheek. That was a great welcome, and he smelled so fucking good. Even after we were seated, his fragrance hung around in my nose. Once seated the conversation flowed and we started to get to know each other a little better. I found out he owns a chain of barbershops, hair salons, and a few nail shops. He was single with no kids, extra plus.

Breakfast was great. I had no complaints at all. Cam wanted to look at some furniture, and with him not being familiar with the city, I took him to a few stores that I loved and helped him find furniture for his condo. All that furniture shopping worked up another appetite, so we ended up doing lunch as well.

Shortly after lunch, we were chilling when his phone rang. Holding up his hand, to let me know he was about to answer, I stopped mid-sentence because I figured it was important.

"What's up, bruh?" he said. I looked off and played in my phone so that I wouldn't be all up in his grill.

"That's fine yeah, I liked the whole area I wouldn't mind buying three suites out of that whole complex if they willing to sell. Aite then bruh, check into that and hit me back," he said and hung up the phone.

"Business looks to be doing good I see?" I said, placing my phone down.

"Yeah, my homie just called and the building we went and looked at this morning had some more vacant spaces. Hell, I want all of that shit," Cam said.

This was a man about his paper and reminded me of Kyron. He did the same thing finding empty places and turning them into things.

"That's good. Make your money. Don't let it make you," I laughed.

Finally, we ended up back at the hotel that Cam was staying at. The room was nice, and he wasn't half-stepping staying in a suite.

"You want something to drink?" he offered.

"Yeah what you got?" I asked.

"Some Moët and Hennessey."

"I'll take Hen," I said.

He poured me a glass of Hen, and we sat out on the terrace of his room. The view of the city was breathtaking, and after a couple of glasses of Hen, my body was on fire. Cam was talking, but I wasn't listening. I had my eyes focused on his lips as they moved so freely. He just didn't know that he had me under a spell. I could no longer restrain myself.

I slowly slid out of the chair that I was sitting on and crawled in between Cam's legs. Cam placed the glass that he held in his hand on the table, and by the look in his eyes, I could tell he was just as hungry as I was. My hands had a mind of their own as they traveled to his shorts and massaged his leg making its way to his third leg and boy was he big. A sly smirk came across my face, and he laughed a little. I think he was calling my bluff. I reached inside his pants and pulled his dick out.

"You gone do that shit out here?" he whispered. I was now massaging his dick with my hands.

"Why would I stop?" I mouthed, looking into his eyes. I lowered my head in his lap and placed him in my mouth. The moan that escaped his lips pushed me to continue. A bitch wasn't trying to be cute. Once I felt him lift my hair and hold it for me, I went to work. He liked it nasty, and I did too. I let his dick touch my tonsils causing me to gag.

"Fuck girl, get up," Cam said out of breath.

Turning me around he placed my hands on the railing of the terrace and kicked my legs apart like he was about to frisk my ass. I could hear the paper from the condom rattling, and without warning, he slid right in me. Here we were bumping and grinding outside for the city to see. Lord, if somebody was watching us, they were getting a good show.

Chapter 7

Waking up from a sex-induced coma, I looked at the clock it was almost nine p.m. *Shit*. My ass had been gone all day and had only talked to Kyron once. It was time for me to get my ass home and quick. I tapped Cam on the shoulder, who looked so peaceful sleeping.

"Hey sleepy head, I got to head up out of here before my man starts flipping, but I enjoyed spending the day with you," I whispered. Cam shifted and sat up

"No problem, I had a wonderful time with you too," Cam leaned in and kissed me on the cheek.

"Hit me up later, aite."

"I sure will." I smiled as I hopped up and started to dress. A bitch really needed to shower, but I couldn't prolong my stay.

On the drive home, I was blasting Mariah Carey's "Always Be My Baby" thinking about Kyron. It felt like every time I fucked off my conscious would be eating away at me. The next thing I know the tears started to fall. *I can't keep doing this*. I really wanted to live a truthful life with Kyron. I promise myself that after tonight, I'm for real done with this shit.

When I got home, I guess Kyron could tell I had been crying. He was really trying to figure out what the hell was wrong with me, but I did what I always did which was lie and shut him out. He hated that shit, and his attitude showed. So, he left all mad and shit. I decided to take the first step and call Cam to let him know what was up. I looked at the clock it was 11:45. Cam answered on the first ring as always.

"What's up, baby?" he sounded good than a motherfucker.

"Cam, don't take this wrong, I really enjoyed myself with you today, but after what happened between us, I just really feel bad, and I can't continue to do this," I cried.

The phone was silent for a minute then finally Cam said something

"Cha Cha I can't do nothing but respect it. I'm just glad we stopped before we started catching feelings because I saw you being the one."

"Well, I guess this is goodbye?" I said, ignoring the last part of what he said.

"We ain't got to be strangers. We can still be sociable."

"Yeah, we can do that. I'm glad you understand, Cam."

"No problem, shawty."

"Bye, Cam."

"Bye, Cha Cha."

Well, that went smoother than I thought.

***

The next couple of months everything had been going great between Kyron and me. I haven't slept with any other man but Kyron. Cam and I spoke occasionally, but that was about it. Tonight, we were going out to celebrate the grand opening of the businesses that Kyron and his friend had just opened. I had heard so much about this guy, but I had never met him. We were all about to hit up Minerva and Kyron were rushing me as usual.

"Baby, you can't rush all this sexiness. You know I don't half step when it comes to you. Don't you want me to represent, baby?" I said seductively.

"Baby, everybody already knows you're sexy as hell." He laughed.

I had on a fitted two-piece dress and a pair of Jimmy Choo wedges. My cousin had installed me a nice platinum blonde wig with wand curls because I was giving my real hair a break. My face was beat to the gods thanks to First Class Lash, so I was ready to make an entrance.

We arrived at Minerva, and when we walked in, all eyes were on us. Kyron had the whole patio area shut down for the event, so everyone was mingling and carrying on conversation. As soon as Kyron walked in, he started getting bombarded. He was that important. Crystal was pulling up, and I needed to go meet her, so I let him know that I was going back outside. Kyron nodded his head and walked over to the cabana. When I got back to the entrance, Crystal was already making her way towards me.

"Hey, girl hey. You look fierce!" she said, taking my hand and spinning me around.

"Thanks, boo. You know I had to show up and show out. Kyron is waiting on us in the cabana," I told her as we headed his way.

Kyron was standing, and I could see him talking to a guy who was decked out in an all-white Gucci fit. The guy's back was facing me, but I could tell he had taste. Kyron looked at me and smiled.

"There you go, baby. You can finally meet my boy and business partner," he said, reaching for my hand. I put my hand in his and turned to lock eyes with what I was hoping was a fucking ghost. No, this couldn't be. Of all motherfucking people, this couldn't be Cam.

"Charisma, this is my nigga, Cam. Cam, this is my girl Charisma," he introduced us. I wanted to die and not come back. Cam and I locked eyes like we were communicating with each other. I waved breaking the stare.

"Nice to meet you. I've heard so much about you," I said.

"Uh yeah, nice to meet you too. You're even prettier than I imagined. Kyron is always talking about you. Now I can finally put a face with a name. Boy Kyron, you got you a keeper. You better keep her close bruh before I steal her," Cam said in a joking manner, but I caught all that shit he was throwing.

We all started laughing, and I signaled for the waitress to order some shots of Patrón.

After downing that Patrón, that shit was running straight through me. I disappeared off to the bathroom. I walked in the bathroom and hurried in the stall. The whole time I was in there, I kept thinking about this bullshit.

Oh my god, I can't fucking believe I slept with somebody that Kyron is close to. I don't think Cam would say anything. We only slept together that one time. Dammit! I got myself together and washed my hands before heading back to the party. When I walked out, Cam was standing there waiting on me

"Cam, what the fuck are you doing, trying to get us caught up?" I whispered.

"Charisma, so that's your name. I can't believe this whole time you were Kyron's girl. The sad thing is I know what we did was wrong, but Kyron isn't a bad guy at all. He's never cheated on you, so why you do this to him? I at least thought maybe you were with a nigga who was doing you dirty but Kyron, he doesn't deserve that," he had the nerve to say.

"Look, Cam. This is neither the place nor the time to discuss this. Don't you think I know what I did was wrong? Why you think I called you and told you we couldn't do this. But don't act like I tried to stop yo ass, you the one didn't care. Look, all I know is I hope you're not going to tell him?" I said.

"Hell nah, this shit going with me to my grave. I hope you just don't want to tell him down the line because your conscious fucking with you. I got a lot of money invested in these businesses with him, and he ain't ever got to know," he said.

"That's fine and to keep everything cool, I think we should stop texting and calling each other also. Matter fact I'm deleting your number now," I said while pulling out my phone and deleting Cam's number out my phone.

"Say no mo," he said.

We both walked out and went our separate ways I found Kyron and finished partying. The remainder of the night was miserable for me. I end up having way too many shots of Patrón and Kyron had to literally carry me out the club.

Chapter 8

Several months had passed, and winter was in full effect. The businesses were booming, and money was coming in full throttle. Kyron and I were at a decent place in our relationship. I haven't talked to Cam on that level since that night we left the club. I would run into him from time to time, and the awkwardness was always there. I wonder does he think about that day we shared. I know I do, but that's a part of my past, and I will not mess things up. I have been doing better than ever with keeping my pussy to myself.

Today I was heading up the road to LaVergne to spend some time with my son. Kyron still had no clue about my secret, but I had planned on telling him real soon. Then all of my demons would be completely out of my life.

When I pulled up to Kase's house, I noticed him and KJ in the yard playing football. When KJ noticed the car, he ran to the car screaming

"Mommy, mommy!" Putting the car in park, I hopped out and ran to my son. KJ jumped in my arms.

"Hey, little man, what you been up to?"

"Nothing much just school, and I hate school," KJ said.

"Oh no, you can't hate school, baby. You got to get your education," I said, looking over at Kase.

"Kase, can you come help get these bags out the car?" I yelled. Kase walked over to the car.

"Cha Cha, I don't know why you keep buying stuff. KJ is good," he huffed.

"One, please don't call me Cha Cha. My name is Charisma, and second, this is my son and if I want to spoil my son, then let me spoil him." I laughed.

We all grabbed the bags and then headed in the house.

"Why are y'all playing outside? It's freezing out there," I said, taking my coat off.

"Cha- I mean Charisma, c'mon we boys. The cold doesn't faze us," Kase said. We walked in the kitchen while KJ went upstairs to look at the things that I had bought him.

"What you got to eat in here?" I asked, walking over to the refrigerator.

"Nothing much. We were gone go grocery shopping today. If you want, we can go grab a bite to eat," Kase suggested.

"Yeah, that's cool. We can go in a minute."

"Charisma, you know the other day KJ asked me why he doesn't live with his mother like the other kids at school does," Kase said, leaning against the counter.

I knew that day would come.

"Wow, I knew he would eventually ask questions. I mean he understands that I love him, but he needs to be raised by you because I can't teach him how to be a man. You know coming up I had no real parenting Kase, so I only did what I thought was right," I wept.

"Charisma, I'm not telling you this to put you on the spot and make you feel bad. It's true that we both have KJ's best interest at heart, but I think now we need to consider you being there even more now," Kase empathized.

This was all hitting me so fast that I couldn't digest it all. I was scared. This is half the reason why I haven't had kids with Kyron because I don't know how to be a mother. I don't want to fail as a mother like my auntie did me. Removing myself from the conversation, I headed upstairs to KJ's room and decided to have a talk with him.

"KJ, come over here and sit down next to mama. I need to talk to you, baby," I said, patting the bed. KJ walked over to sit down next to me. He was so handsome that I sometimes shock myself knowing I contributed in making a human being.

"What's up, mama?" he said, sounding like a little man.

"I heard you asked your father why you don't live with me?" KJ nodded his head.

"See, mama had you when I was only seventeen. I barely had a place to stay, and I was in school. So, your dad and I felt it was best that you live with him so that I could finish school and go to college. Your daddy has always been a little well off in the financial area, so he could give you things that I couldn't give you in life. You know your father paid for me to go to college. If it wasn't for him, ain't no telling what I would be doing with my life. I couldn't teach you how to be a man and all those things, but I made sure I stayed around so that I wouldn't miss out on anything. However, soon I think you will finally be able to come stay with me. Your dad and I will work something out to where you can live with both of us," I told KJ.

"Well, can't you just move in with daddy?" KJ asked.

"It's not that simple, son. Mommy has a boyfriend whose name is Kyron, and whether you tell me or not, I know your dad has a girlfriend. I'm not dumb," I said, and we both laughed. KJ and I hugged, and I kissed him on the cheek.

"Now get your coat on, we finna make daddy take us to eat," I told him.

While KJ got ready, I left out of his room and made my way down the hall towards Kase's room. Peeking inside, I saw that Kase was on the phone looking out the window.

"She never stays the night, Lisa. She comes to spend time with our son. I don't understand you. Damn, are you jealous?" he said. I walked in the room and made my presence known, and he turned around

"We're ready to go eat, Kase," I said with my hands on my hip. He signaled for me to hold on.

"Lisa, look. I don't have time for this. You're starting to stress me out. I'll holler at you later," he said and hung up the phone.

"The funny thing is I just told your son that I knew you had a girlfriend, and I wasn't dumb." I laughed.

"How y'all get on me having a girlfriend?" he asked.

"Because he asked why I don't just move in with y'all," I said. Kase walked over to me and put his arm around me

"If you did, I would drop her just to have you back again. You know I've always loved you, Charisma. I've never allowed my heart to even love another woman. I blame myself for taking advantage of you when you were younger and screwing your life up. I know you have a hard time now fighting your demons, but I really want you to know that I'm sorry, and I hope you forgive me," Kase pleaded.

I never heard him speak like that. I tried to hold back tears, but they just wouldn't stop flowing.

"Kase, I forgave you a long time ago. I had to fight my own demons and was strong enough to finally not let them control my life. I'm just glad that you've been here and every time I needed you, you were here with open arms, and I will always love you for that," I cried. KJ came running in the room with his coat on

"Y'all ready? I'm starving," he said. We both looked at him and laughed.

"C'mon, little nigga," Kase said. We all hopped in the car, and I got in the back seat with KJ because he wanted me to watch a movie with him.

"Where y'all want to eat at?" Kase turned around and asked.

"McDonald's!" screamed KJ.

I gave Kase a nod to let him know that I was fine with that. Kase started the car and pulled off, KJ and I were watching the *Lego* movie on the DVD player. I had just texted Kyron to see what he was doing and told him I loved him and would see him later. Kase was nodding his head to the music trying to look all cool. I was cracking up at him. I turned to look out the window. We were sitting at the red light. The light turned green, and Kase started to pull off when I saw another truck flying through because the truck ran the red light.

"Kase lookout!" I screamed.

Kase turned to look, but it was too late. The truck hit us at full speed, and that's all I remember before blacking out.

Chapter 9

Opening my eyes, I was dazed and confused as I looked around the white room. The smell of sanitizing products and the beeping of the machine let me know that I was at the hospital. Panic settled in as I moved my hands over my body. Hold up. I can feel my body parts. I can feel my arms, feet, and legs. I didn't see any bandages, so why am I laying in the hospital? That's when it hit me. Oh no! Where's KJ and Kase? That's when I looked over in the chair, and I noticed Kyron sleeping. Jesus, this can't be happening. I wanted to go back to sleep and not wake up.

"Kyron," I whispered.

He opened his eyes, which were bloodshot red. I could tell he had been crying. He got up and walked over to the bed. I started panicking

"Kyron what's going on, where's KJ and Kase?" I asked. Kyron didn't reply. He just hit the nurse's button and asked for the doctor. The doctor walked in and neared the bed.

"Nice to see you awake, Ms. Johnson."

"Doctor, where is my son and Kasey? Are they ok?" I asked not even giving a fuck that Kyron was standing there with a permanent mug on his face. I was starting to freak out.

"Look, Ms. Johnson. It's critical that you remain calm. You have some internal bleeding and blood pressure problems that we need to keep stabilized. Now, your son is fine. His seat belt and you shielding him is what saved his life. He just got a few cuts from shattered glass, and that's it. Now Mr. Woods, on the other hand, I'm sorry to tell you this, but he didn't make it. He was ejected from the car and loss too much blood before he even made it to the hospital. I'm so sorry for your loss," the doctor said solemnly.

"Nooooooo!" I wailed.

"This can't be. What am I supposed to do about KJ?" I put my head in my hands and just continued to cry.

"I'll leave you two alone," the doctor said, leaving the room. I lifted my head, and I looked at Kyron trying to read him. Finally, Kyron said something.

"Were you cheating on me with this nigga Kasey whatever his name is?" he asked calmly. I was taken aback with how he flat out disrespected Kasey name.

"No, I wasn't. I knew this day would come and I had planned on telling you, but I didn't think it would be under these conditions. When I was sixteen, my mama died left me with my auntie, and I met Kase. He was twenty-two. He basically took my virginity, and I got pregnant. We agreed that he would raise KJ so that I could finish school and college. We were actually agreeing upon letting KJ come and live with me right before the accident."

"What I don't understand is why in the fuck you would keep having a child a secret? Damn, did you think I wouldn't accept him?" he said angrily.

"I wasn't worried about you not accepting him. I had some things that I was dealing with that was keeping me from getting my own child. I just feared that I was gone fail him!" I yelled.

"So, you and his father wasn't messing around?" Kyron asked.

"No, in no kind of way," I said. Kyron paced the floor like he was trying to walk a hole in it.

"Charisma, I feel like I don't even know who the fuck you are. You have been living two different lives. I don't even know what to think." He was full of rage.

"Kyron, I'm sorry. I swear I am. Please don't do this!" I pleaded. Kyron kissed me on the forehead and walked out of the room without saying one word to me.

"Kyron, wait!" I called out, but he just kept walking.

My life was officially falling apart. I had lost the father of my child, and the love of my life. Moments later there was a knock on the door and in came KJ and Kase's mother. I just burst out crying all over again.

"Oh no baby, don't you do it," Kase mother said, rushing straight the bed.

"Mommy, don't cry. G-Ma said daddy is in an even better place than here," KJ consoled me.

"You are your daddy's child. How can you be so little yet have the strength of a man?" I said, hugging KJ.

"Charisma, now baby, I know you and Kase were on good terms and y'all did the best raising my grandson. Kase told me how much he loved you and KJ, and how he messed up your life," his mother said.

I thought back to the conversation that Kase and I had standing in his bedroom that day, and I smiled.

"Now, I'm too old to be raising a child, and I know you will do right by your son," she said.

"Of course, I will I wouldn't dare let him out my sight. KJ, do you want to come live with mama when I get out of the hospital?" I asked him.

"Yes, ma'am!" KJ jumped up and down.

"Well, we're going to go and let you get some rest, ok baby?" Kase mom said. I admired her strength because for her to lose her child, she was being strong in front of KJ.

"Okay, talk to you guys later." I watched as KJ and his granny walked out of the room.

Laying my head back on the pillow, I stared up at the ceiling reliving the accident— Kase smiling and carrying on, KJ excited to be in the presence of both parents, and those heartfelt words Kase said not knowing that would be the last time we shared a moment like that. All this was killing me. Grabbing ahold of the blanket, I pulled it up to my mouth and bit down on it letting out a gut-wrenching scream. My mind kept running back to Kyron and the way I had betrayed him. I felt bad.

If he knew how many times I cheated on him with other men, he would never forgive me. What am I supposed to do?

Chapter 10

Two days later, I was released from the hospital. My home felt empty. I was waiting for KJ's arrival, and I couldn't wait to see my son. He had ridden with his uncle to get his things from his dad's. I told them they could do that because I didn't want to step foot back in that house. I couldn't deal with the memories. I haven't heard from Kyron since he left the hospital, I tried calling and texting, but he wasn't responding to me. I knew he had been here, and he packed up a few things. I wasn't sure if he was leaving for a while, or if he was coming back to get the rest of his things.

Shortly after, I heard a truck pulling up in the driveway. I went to the window, and I saw it was KJ and his uncle, so I opened the door to greet them.

"Welcome to your new home, KJ!"

"Where's my room, mommy?" he asked, running in the house.

"Go upstairs and find it," I smiled. I turned to Kase's brother, Kory.

"Thank you for setting up his room while I was in the hospital. I really appreciate it," I told him.

"No problem, I just wanted a smooth transition for my nephew," Kory said. Kory finished moving the rest of KJ things in the house.

***

It was kind of hard getting used to having KJ at first, but eventually, things started to get better. After Kase's funeral, I think it really hit KJ that his daddy was really gone. I had to get both him and me into some counseling. It had been almost three months since I had seen or spoke to Kyron. I don't know where his ass was.

It was a Sunday afternoon, and I was doing my typical cleaning and Mariah Carey's "Always Be My Baby" came on the radio. I fell to my knees and started crying. Those words stung as they came blasting out the stereo.

♫*And we'll linger on. Time can't erase a feeling so strong. No way you're never gone shake me, ooh darling cause you'll always be my baby.*♫

The first person that came to mind was Cam. Why didn't I think to call him? I ran over and grabbed my phone off the kitchen counter and dialed Cam's number. *Come on, Cam. Pick up.*

"Ugh, fucking voicemail!" I said and slammed the phone down. *Think Charisma. Think.* I picked up the phone again and dialed Cam's number.

"Hello," Cam said all raspy and shit.

"Cam, I'm sorry to wake you, even though you should be up seeing that it is two in the afternoon," I said.

"Who the hell is this?" he snapped.

"Charisma boy, get up. Look, I really need to talk to you. Are you busy today?" I asked.

"I didn't have any plans."

"Well, can you be at my house around five for dinner?"

"Uh, Charisma, I don't think that's a good idea," he said.

"Look, Cam. This is not a pleasure call. I really need to talk to you about, Kyron," I said. There was a brief silence on the phone.

"Well, are you coming or not?"

"Yeah, I'll be there, girl," he said and hung up the phone. It was so crazy how he acts like he was never feeling a bitch.

I finished cleaning the house and good thing I decided to cook today, so my dinner was almost finished. KJ came running in the kitchen

"KJ, what I tell you about running in the kitchen, what if you fall and bust that big head of yours?" I called out.

"Sorry mama, what's for dinner?" KJ asked.

"Chicken and dressing, mac and cheese, and turnip greens," I replied. KJ started rubbing his belly.

"Help me set the table," I insisted. KJ and I started doing just that.

I looked at the clock and noticed it was almost five, so I rushed upstairs and changed into a pair of sweat pants and a wife beater, trying to look unattractive as possible to Cam. By the time I got changed and combed my hair down from being wrapped, the doorbell rang.

"Mommy, somebody's at the door!" KJ yelled.

"I hear it, sweetie, I got it," I said, coming down the stairs.

When I opened the door, Cam was standing there in almost the same thing I had on, some gray sweatpants and a t-shirt. I laughed to myself because he probably was trying to do the same thing. I was doing by not trying to turn on the other, even though he failed miserably with the gray sweatpants.

"Hey Cam, it's nice to see you again," I said, hugging him.

"Sup Charisma, I see you got it smelling good up in here," he said while walking into the house.

Closing the door, I showed him into the dining room where we had set the table. KJ came walking up to me

"Is it time to eat, mommy?" he asked.

"Yes baby, go wash your hands." Cam looked at KJ and then looked at me.

"Mommy? I thought you didn't have any kids? He's not Kyron's is he?" he asked curiously.

"Yeah mommy, and no he's not Kyron's. My son is seven, and me and Kyron only been together for two years."

"Wait. Kyron didn't tell you I had a son?" I asked. Cam sat down at the table across from me.

"Honestly, he really didn't go into details with me about what happened between y'all. He's just been focusing on making this money." Cam shrugged.

"Well, after dinner I guess I have to tell you everything," I said.

KJ came back in the dining room, and we said grace and started to eat. Cam was hitting it off with KJ, and shockingly, KJ was accepting. Watching him interact with someone other than his father melted my heart. I just wish that was with Kyron and not Cam.

After dinner, KJ went to take his bath and then he went into his room to play the game. Cam and I went into the living room to have a seat. That's when I told him everything as to how I met KJ's dad, why KJ was living with his dad, and my cheating ass ways. I basically told him everything, even about the wreck and how Kase died.

"Damn girl, I'm gone need a drink after all that," Cam said.

"I haven't heard or seen Kyron since the day he walked out of the hospital. I mean I have texted him, tried calling, trying to see at least where we stand, but he refuses to answer me. Shit, how much time he needs?"

"Look, Kyron loves you, and he will come around. I just hope it ain't too late and somebody done got a hold of you." Cam smiled. I caught that and shook my head. Cam will always be Cam no matter how hard he fronted.

We continued to talk and were sipping on some Moët when I heard the front door open. I got up to see what it was making sure KJ hadn't opened the door. I couldn't believe this shit.

"Kyron, what are you doing here?"

Chapter 11

Kyron stood there with an unpleasant look on his face. This was all too much.

"So, for three months I have been riding past this house every single day. I ride by at night when I think you're sleeping to make sure no other cars are in the driveway. Tonight, I drive by, and I see my nigga's truck in the driveway. I've been waiting for four motherfucking hours to see when this nigga was gone come out the house, but instead, I walk in and y'all sipping Moët looking cozy. I've been out here feeling bad for leaving like I did, and you turn around and getting close with my nigga!" Kyron spat with so much venom.

Cam stood up.

"Nah bruh, it ain't even what you think."

"First of all, Kyron, I don't appreciate you coming in here acting like you running things, and I haven't seen you in three months. Secondly, I am not fucking your nigga, and I'm appalled that you would even accuse me of such a thing," I said.

"Go head Charisma, tell me some more of your lies," Kyron seethed, rolling his eyes like a little bitch.

See, I know this fool had lost his fucking mind. Clearly, he got the right bitch. I stood directly in his face.

"So, why the fuck is you here if you not willing to hear what I have to say since you keep thinking I'm telling lies. Huh? I've been sitting here for three months going through hell, stressed out, and not knowing if I was gone get you back or not. I'm trying to raise my son, not to mention who is going through things because he lost his father, remember. The last thing on my mind is fucking another nigga, so you can turn around and walk the fuck back out of my door if you think I'm finna argue with you. Now, I called Cam over here for dinner so that I could talk to him about us. I was trying to see if he had at least spoken to you about us, and him not knowing much, after dinner I told him my whole fucking life story that led up to today!" I yelled as Kyron stood there looking like a lost little puppy.

Cam had walked back over to pour him a drink, and I turned to walk upstairs.

Before I headed up, I turned around saying one last thing. "Now, I'm going to tuck my son in bed. If you want to talk about things, I'll be back. If not, you can leave right now."

When I got upstairs to KJ's room, opening the door a smile crept on my face. After that heavy dinner, I knew he wouldn't be able to stay up long. I'm kind of glad that he fell asleep on the game so that he wasn't able to hear the shouting match downstairs. I removed his headset from his head and turned the game off. Picking his heavy ass up, I laid him in the bed and tucked him in. This mommy thing was coming along well. Leaning down, I kissed him on his forehead.

When I came back downstairs from tucking KJ in, Kyron and Cam were sitting on the couch with an opened bottle of Patrón. Oh my God, tonight was going to be a long night, so I guess I'll join the party.

Walking over to the bar, I retrieved a shot glass and poured me two shots.

"Damn Charisma, you good?" Cam laughed.

"I spoke with Cam while you were upstairs, and he told me everything. I'm sorry I even doubted y'all. It's just that after that stuff happened, my trust been a little fucked up," Kyron admitted. I was starting to feel the shots of Patrón.

"I don't want to go back in this relationship questioning each other and what we've been doing, Kyron. All this stuff needs to be put behind us."

"Well, let's put everything out on the table now. Something like an honesty box. Once we tell each other what we got to say it's never to be discussed ever again after tonight. We can move on from there," Kyron threw out there.

I'm thinking to myself *not no fucking honesty box*, I stood up and walked back over to the bar fridge and pulled out another bottle of Patrón.

"Bruh, you might as well start rolling up that loud and get some more liquor in your system. You sure you want to do the honesty box?" Cam asked Kyron. I looked at Cam like *what the fuck you doing nigga*.

"Hell yeah, we both move on with a clean slate no matter how bad it might be. Give me that Patrón," Kyron said, grabbing the bottle and turning it up.

After we smoked about three blunts and drank more Patrón, it was time for this honesty shit. I looked at Kyron.

"Well go head and hit me with the bullshit." I sighed.

"Nah, ladies first, it's only right," Kyron teased. I gave him an ill ass look.

"How about I ask you a question, and we go from there then?" Kyron threw in.

"That's fine." I looked over at Cam he was high as a kite, but I can tell this nigga was worried not knowing what was about to go down.

"Have you ever cheated on me during the two years we been together?" Kyron asked.

Damn, he just went in for the kill on the first damn question. This shit was going to take more alcohol. I got up and stumbled over to the bar. Damn, we were out of Patrón, so I popped open the 1800, taking a shot.

"Damn, is it that bad baby?" Kyron questioned. I turned around to face the music.

"Yes, I cheated on you with two people during our relationship. Now when I met you Kase and I was never together, but we would fuck around every now and then. That lasted about four months when we first started dating only because I didn't know if you and I were going to get serious like we did. When I saw we were going to be together, I cut it off with him altogether. I never touched him again," I whispered.

I looked at Kyron who amazingly didn't look surprised. Cam, on the other hand, looked like he was about to shit himself. He stood up and walked over to the bar and turned up the Tequila.

"Y'all niggas sho is drinking a lot. Cam, nigga, you over there sweating like you in the hot seat," Kyron said, laughing.

"Nah, I'm good, bruh." Cam let out a nervous chuckle.

"Well to finish my story the second person I slept with was…"

Cam started pacing the floor and scratching his head nervously.

"…the second person I slept with was this guy name Taye." I lied, twisting the truth.

Now I was not about to tell Kyron that I had slept with Cam. Some things should remain untold, and that will go to the grave with me. I looked at Cam, and he winked at me.

"I messed with him for about two months, but come to find out, Bria had got her hands on him as well, which was part of the reason why I beat her ass at the park that day. That's basically it. I haven't been intimate or talked to another man since then. I have no other outside children, I'm not married, and Cha Cha is dead," I said, letting out a sigh of relief.

"Cha Cha, who the hell is Cha Cha?" Kyron asked.

"That was my name I used with the other guys. I only allowed you to call me Charisma, so now your turn," I told Kyron while taking another shot.

I needed to stop because I was seeing double already. Cam walked over and sat down on the couch and sat next to Kyron.

"Well, I cheated on you twice. That night Bria came over to do my hair, we fucked," Kyron admitted.

Man, you talking about seeing red. I wanted to paint the room with Kyron's blood. This motherfucker had his audacity. Funky bitch. The room started spinning, and I fell on the couch between Cam and Kyron.

"I knewww you slept with that b-b-bitch," I slurred and smacked him in the back of the head.

"Calm down, Charisma," Kyron said, grabbing my hand.

"Who was the other bitch?" I asked.

"Well, like two days later before Bria left town, me and Cam both smashed her," Kyron nervously said. I turned to look at Cam.

"Ohhh Cam, you got some secrets too?" I asked, trying to stand up but fell back down on the couch.

"Charisma, it wasn't like that," he said, trying to defend himself. Kyron put his arms around me and said, "Baby, we were drunk. That bitch started—" I interrupted Kyron.

"Save me the fucking details. You better be lucky that bitch is gone because I will have that hoe dead right now!" I spat.

"That's exactly why I didn't tell you, you probably would've had Cam and me knocked off to," he said.

"Well, I guess karma's a bitch." I shrugged.

Kyron stood up from the couch, and I noticed he winked at Cam. I was drunk, but I knew something was up with these niggas. Kyron picked me up off the couch and carried me towards the steps.

"Where are you taking me?" I slurred with my head tucked on Kyron's chest.

I could hear Cam walking up the stairs behind us. When we entered the bedroom, Cam had a duffle bag. He opened the bag and poured all the money out on the bed that was in the bag. That's when Kyron laid me on the bed on top of all the money. The damn room was spinning like the wheel on *Wheel of Fortune*. What happened next, I wasn't expecting. I felt my body being rubbed down by four hands. This shit wasn't right, but I couldn't move, and the shit felt good. I would never forget Cam's touch.

The next thing you know I was getting fucked and sucked by both Kyron and Cam. This shit was something that I told Kyron about when we first started dating when I was on my freak shit. He asked me what's my fantasy, and I told him making love on a bed of money to the man that I plan on marrying and another nigga with just as much money as the man I'm marrying. A bitch was just money hungry. See, he should've known then that I was gone be a problem. He remembered my fantasy and made it come true. So, maybe this was a sign. Maybe he planned on popping the question soon.

Chapter 12

I woke up the next day feeling like shit. Plus, I was the only person in the bed. *KJ! Oh no, he was supposed to be at school.* Looking at the clock, it was 11:30. Frantically, I hopped out of bed and ran to KJ's room. Opening the door, KJ was gone. I ran downstairs, and Kyron was sitting in the living room watching ESPN.

"Where's KJ?" I asked, startling him. Kyron turned around.

"He's at school. I knew you wasn't gone be able to get him up in time, so I got him ready for school. You know I got to get used to this daddy shit," Kyron said.

I smiled at Kyron and strutted over to him giving him a hug and a kiss.

"Thank you, baby. You know last night at first I thought y'all niggas were on some other shit, but then I put shit together and realized you remembered my fantasy."

"You sure that's something you felt comfortable doing with Cam though?"

"Cam is like my brother. He is the only nigga I really trust. You see how much money I done invested with this nigga and how much he done made us. Plus, he the only nigga I know with a little bit more money than me." Kyron laughed.

I laid my head on Kyron's chest.

"Baby, I'm happy that we put everything behind us and was able to move forward with our lives."

"Me too, baby."

"Baby, last night you were on it and freaky as hell. I think you slick enjoyed having Cam in the bedroom with us," Kyron said. I lifted my head to make eye contact. I gave him the *are you serious* look.

"I rarely even remember last night," I said, putting it off.

I wasn't about to admit to anything, and I stand on my word of keeping that secret to myself. No way would I tell my man his friend's sex was better than his was.

***

It was almost time for KJ to get out of school, so I went upstairs and hopped in the shower. I stood in the shower a good twenty minutes thinking about what Kyron said. I was trying to act like I wasn't enjoying it, but I was. Cam's sex game was mind-blowing. I know Cam enjoyed that shit. I laughed to myself thinking about it. I hopped out the shower and threw on something to get KJ.

While standing on the bus stop, I decided to call Crystal, but the hoe didn't answer, and that was weird. KJ's bus approached, and he jumped off the bus.

"Hey boy, how was your day today?" I asked.

"It was fun. We really didn't do too much. Mama, I like Kyron. He and I had a talk this morning," he said quickly.

"Y'all did?"

"Yeah, he was like he was sorry about what happened to my daddy, and that he was just going to pick up where my daddy left off and raise me like I'm his son. He said I didn't have to call him daddy unless I felt like I wanted to," KJ said.

I smiled and thought yeah, I got a keeper. My phone started ringing and interrupted our convo. I looked down, and it was Crystal calling me back.

"Oh, so now you want to call back trick. What nigga got you all hemmed up?" I asked.

"Shut up, but if you must know, I have been seeing somebody."

"Girl, shut up, and why haven't I met him or hell even heard about him?"

"You gone meet him, and you have seen him before. He's one of Kyron's friends."

"Who?" I stopped dead in my tracks.

"You know Kyron's homeboy Cam," she said.

I almost dropped my fucking phone. This shit couldn't possibly be happening. What the fuck kind of nasty fucking everybody shit was this.

"Hello," she said.

"Yeah, I'm here, girl. I was listening to KJ, um let me call you right back," I said and hung up the phone. KJ and I walked into the house.

"Go get out your uniform and get started on your homework if you have any," I told him.

Kyron was laid out, so I went upstairs and called Cam.

"Wassup Charisma, you calling about last night?" he said with a slight chuckle.

"Fuck no, my nigga. I'm calling because you're dating Crystal, my best friend. Why would you go their last night if you were messing with her? I ain't with that messy shit, Cam. That's my best friend," I whispered.

"I didn't think it would be a big deal, that's just another one of our secrets, Charisma," he said. This nigga was playing games. I just hung the phone up in his face. Ugh! I was beyond irritated.

Chapter 13

Two months had passed, and it was officially summer. The heat was working my nerves. I had been irritable as hell lately. We had been doing a lot of double dating as well. I had kind of grew to accept Cam and Crystal, but deep down inside, I still didn't approve of the relationship. He couldn't smash the homie. What irritated me more was Cam was a decent guy, and when he was involved with someone, he didn't play. Crystal, on the other hand, she was like I used to be. She was playing Cam so fucking hard that it was pitiful.

I had just dropped KJ off at the shop with Kyron and was headed to the shop to work on a client. I made a quick stop at Starbuck's before heading to the shop. When I got to the shop, I noticed some regulars that were here for their standing appointments.

"Morning y'all," I spoke to everybody.

Heading into the office, I locked my purse and stuff up and headed back to the floor. My mind was on getting started and getting out of here as fast as I could. I wasn't in a talkative mood today.

"You ok, girl? You look like shit?" Crystal asked.

"I feel like shit," I replied. I took my work seriously, and I wasn't about to rush, but I couldn't finish my client head fast enough. I just wanted to lay down.

***

A couple of hours had passed, and I was finally done and headed home. I know I did a whole 80 mph home. I pulled up in the driveway and saw both Cam and Kyron's car there. *Fuck! I don't want to be bothered.* I got out of the car and headed in the house.

"What's up, baby?"

"Hey, baby," I mumbled. I walked into the kitchen, got me a Sprite out the refrigerator, and grabbed a slice of pizza that I'd seen sitting on the counter.

"You aite, Charisma, you don't look so well?" Kyron asked. No sooner than I could respond, I threw up everywhere.

"Fuck!" I yelled. Both Kyron and Cam looked at each other then turned to look at me.

"Baby, you sure you ok? You ain't been yourself lately."

"I just want to lay down," I said and quickly headed to the bedroom. After brushing my teeth and getting out of these work clothes, I climbed in bed. Kyron came upstairs.

"Baby I hate seeing you like this. You rarely get sick."

"I'm fine baby, just let me rest a little bit," I groaned.

Kyron walked out of the room and closed the door. I laid there thinking about how I been feeling lately— sore breasts, irritable, nauseated. Oh my god! I haven't had a period in months. I smacked myself on the forehead. *Damn Charisma, how could you not notice?* Oh no, wait a minute. Did Kyron and Cam use condoms the night that we had a threesome? We were all so drunk that I seriously doubt it.

"ARRGHHH!" I let out a scream intended for nobody to hear, but both Kyron and Cam came running in the room.

"What's wrong, you ok baby?" Kyron questioned.

"I didn't realize that I had screamed that loud. I was thinking about something sorry."

"Cam, can you excuse us for a minute?" I asked Cam.

"Yeah, no problem," Cam said as he exited the room.

"Baby, I think you need to run to the store and get me a pregnancy test," I said calmly. Kyron eyes got huge.

"Yo, you serious right now baby? Don't be playing with me. You know I've been waiting on this moment for a while now!" he exclaimed.

"I'm so serious, babe. I haven't had a period in two months, and it explains all the other symptoms I've been having now that I think about it. Baby, here's an important question. Um, the night we had the threesome, did y'all use protection?" I asked.

Kyron looked around and started fondling with his dreads thinking.

"Fuck baby! I don't think we did. Well, I know I didn't I can't speak on Cam," he mentioned.

I couldn't believe this shit. Here I was possibly pregnant and didn't know if I was carrying Kyron or Cam's baby. Fuck my life. Kyron walked out of the room and then returned with Cam.

"Bruh, that night do you remember if you used a condom?" Kyron asked him.

"What, don't tell me you're pregnant, Charisma?" Cam asked.

"I'm not sure yet. I asked Kyron to get me a test. I do know I haven't had a period in two months."

"This is some messed up shit. I don't remember shit from that night," Cam said. I was starting to get pissed off.

"Well, don't just stand there. Go get me a test!" I screamed. They both ran out of the room.

Chapter 14

I couldn't believe I was standing here looking at both pregnancy tests that read *positive*. I already felt that I was pregnant anyway, but now I had the stress of dealing with who the fuck was the father of the child I was carrying. I swear my life consists of getting fucked up by the day. I knew Kyron and Cam was standing on the other side of the door. It was so quiet out there you could hear a pin drop. Opening the door, I walked out of the bathroom.

"So what the test say?" Kyron asked.

"Positive." It got quiet again.

"Baby, I've been waiting on this moment for so long, I'm truly happy," Kyron said.

"I'm happy that I could make you happy," I mumbled, but I wasn't in the best mood.

"Well I'm happy for both of you, but I don't really know how to feel about this seeing that it could be my baby as well," Cam interrupted.

I kind of felt where Cam was coming from or did I really?

***

Later that evening I was chilling at home alone. Kyron and KJ had left to go to the mall and out to eat. Kyron made it his priority to do father-son dates with KJ, and I loved that about him. I decided to try and get some much-needed rest. My phone started ringing. I ignored it and let it go to voicemail. A couple of minutes later it rang again, I looked at the phone, and it was Cam. *Ugh, what did he want?*

"What Cam?" I blew out in frustration.

"Sorry Charisma, were you sleeping?" he asked.

"I sort of was trying to get a little rest while the boys were gone. What's up?"

"I'm having mixed emotions about this pregnancy thing. What if the baby you carrying is mine?" he questioned.

I sat up in bed.

"Cam, I'm really not trying to think negative about the situation, what if it is yours, that doesn't mean we gone be together. This will just be one of them situations where you would take care of your child and be in his life fully because Kyron wouldn't keep you from your child. We are all facing the consequences of a dumb ass choice we all made. That's just something we're gone have to deal with accordingly."

"Do you want this baby to be your baby, Cam?" I asked curiously.

"I want a child, but I also want to marry and be with my child's mother, and I know that's not gone happen, so honestly no," he said.

"Cam, stop stressing and think positive. I don't think God would bring me and Kyron back together to stir up a problem between us now." I laughed.

"I guess you've got a point, girl. Well, I just wanted to talk to you about the situation, so I'll let you get back to getting your rest," Cam said.

"Aite Cam, take care."

So much for getting any rest, after getting off the phone with Cam, I just couldn't seem to go back to sleep. I decided to get up and fix me something to eat and see if I could keep something down now. I warmed me up leftovers from the other night and sat down at the kitchen table. I decided to give Crystal a call. I dialed Crystal's number and waited for her to answer

"Hello" she sang into the phone.

"Hey girl, what are you doing?"

"Nothing girl just laying here with Cam watching some movie."

This nigga was laid up with her and had the nerve to just get off the phone with me.

"Aw well, I was calling to tell you the good news, if you haven't already heard."

"What news. Oh god."

"You're going to be another God mommy. I found out I was pregnant today," I said.

"Oh my gosh, congrats girl. I know Kyron is fucking happy."

"Girl, happy ain't the word. I got to call and schedule me a doctor's appointment tomorrow so that I can see how far along I am."

"Yeah, girl you need to get on that and keep me updated with everything. I'm finna head over to Clarissa's house in a few. I may swing by there."

This hoe wasn't no good. Clarissa was another one of her little pieces.

"You and these code names, girl. So you're still messing with Clarence? I don't know why you just don't choose a guy and stick with him. Cam is a nice guy. He would do you better than Clarence ass, but you're grown and gone do you regardless."

"Exactly, but we will discuss this another time. I'll talk to you later," Crystal said quickly.

"Bye girl," I said and hung up the phone.

She gone get enough of fooling around on Cam. I'm not gone get involved in the mix. It ain't my place.

Chapter 15

A couple of weeks passed, and Kyron and I were sitting here in the doctor's room waiting for me to get my exam. When the nurse entered the room, I kind of got nervous thinking back to when I was pregnant with KJ.

"Ms. Johnson, I just need to ask you a couple of questions if you don't mind," the nurse said.

"Ok," I replied.

"Do you happen to remember the first day of your last period?" she asked.

I nodded and told her the date.

"Ok," she said handing me a slip of paper. I glanced down at the paper and noticed an estimated date of conception.

"Excuse me. This estimated date of conception how accurate is that?" I asked.

"It's pretty accurate if not the exact date. It's a couple of days before or after that day you got pregnant on."

"Oh ok, thank you," I said.

"No problem, the doctor will be in shortly." I turned to Kyron smiling and handing him the sheet of paper.

"What are you smiling for, baby?" he asked.

"Look at the date, baby. That date is the week after the date we had the you know what with Cam, baby. I can tell you the night I got pregnant, and it most definitely wasn't that night," I said, Kyron looked at me with the biggest smile on his face.

We both were relieved. Boy, I couldn't be happier now that I knew for a fact that the child I was carrying was Kyron's and not Cam's.

As soon as we left the doctor's office, Kyron called and told Cam the news. I knew he had to be relieved. Now he can go on with his life and not confuse ours or our child. Well, based on the info that the doctor gave us, I'll be due in mid-December. Kyron was dead set on having a girl since he felt he had a son in KJ. I fear having a little girl honestly. I fear that she grows up and take after me. I knew nothing about raising a little girl.

Two Months Later

Today was the day that Kyron and I would find out what we were having, and the day Crystal was throwing our gender reveal. I thought it was a great idea, but the anticipation was killing me. We were allowed to go to the doctor, but instead of the doctor telling us right then and there what we were having, she had to put the sex in a sealed envelope, and we weren't allowed to open it until the dinner tonight. We walked into the doctor's office and were greeted by the nurses. Once back in the room, the ultrasound process began.

"So you guys are doing a gender reveal. I think that is so neat. Well, we are going to look and at least see if everything is progressing right with the baby, and see if the baby is healthy," the doctor told us.

I looked over at Kyron who had the biggest smile on his face.

"Well by the looks of things this child is very healthy and growing correctly to term, which is good news," the doctor said. She then printed out the ultrasound and stepped out of the room.

Kyron and I waited patiently for the doctor to return. Shortly after that, the doctor walked into the room and handed me the sealed envelope.

"Well, I hope you guys are happy with what's in the envelope."

"Thank you, Doc, we'll see you next time." I smiled and held the envelope.

When we left the doctor, it was time for Kyron and me to go our separate ways so that we could get ready for our dinner tonight. I drove to the nail spa so I could get me a mani and pedi. While I was getting my toes done, I just so happened to be looking out the window, and I could've sworn I seen a car that looked just like Bria's pull in the lot. That couldn't have been her though. I ain't seen her since the fight, and I heard she left town. I brushed the thought off quickly and continued to enjoy this pedicure.

About forty-five minutes later, I was finally leaving the nail spa. I then went over to Green Hills to pick up my dress and shoes. I called Crystal to see how everything was running and to inform her of what I was doing. When I arrived at the store to get my dress, I had to try it on to make sure it fit perfectly. The dress looked lovely. It was a coral, strapless dress with a v-cut sheer layered flow to show my legs. Then I had the perfect pair of wedges to go with it.

When I pulled up at the house, I noticed Kyron hadn't made it home yet. KJ was at his granny's; she was bringing him later. I got out of the car, ran into the house, and went ahead and took my shower so that would be one less thing that I had to do. I got out the shower and was finna oil my body but realized I had left my bag of goodies I bought from Victoria Secret on the couch in the living room. Running downstairs, I wasn't expecting Kyron and Cam to be sitting there rolling a blunt.

"Oh shit!" I squealed, trying to cover my private parts with my hands. Kyron and Cam turned around looking dead at me. I ducked behind the wall and peeped my head out

"I thought I was in the house alone. Kyron, can you pass me that bag on the couch, please?" I asked.

"Didn't you hear us down here?" Kyron asked with a hint of attitude bringing me the bag.

"If I would've heard y'all down here I would've told you to bring me the bag. Don't start no shit tonight," I said, snatching the bag and walking back upstairs.

When I got back upstairs, I continued to get dressed. My phone dinged, and it was my cousin Sha telling me she was about to pull up. I sat down at the vanity so that I would be ready when she walked in. I could hear Sha making her way upstairs.

"Hey girl, oh my god! You look so adorable, well sexier honey to be pregnant." She gasped.

"Thanks, ladybug."

Sha got started on my hair and makeup. About forty-five minutes later, I looked at the time, and it was about time to head out and be on our way.

When I got downstairs, Kyron was dressed and standing at the bar making a drink. I cleared my throat getting his attention when I walked in the room. Kyron turned around.

"You seriously trying to get wasted for our dinner tonight Kyron?" I asked jokingly.

"Nah baby, I'm just a little nervous. You look so damn sexy right now." He smiled and licked his lips.

"I know you not nervous about the sex of the baby, and thanks, baby." Kyron turned the drink up and grabbed my hand

"You ready to get this show on the road, fat mama?" he asked, giving me a twirl.

"Hahaha fat mama, really? Boy, c'mon." I laughed.

We arrived at The Oak Steakhouse where we had an area for our guests. Crystal had everything set up nicely. All our close friends and family were there. Everyone was trying to rub my belly and telling me how gorgeous I was. When we got up to our table, Kyron was already on drink number three. Don't ask me why this nigga was drinking like this. I just tried to ignore it because I didn't want to cause a scene. Everyone had finally arrived and was seated, Crystal walked up front and grabbed the microphone.

"Hey everybody, for those of you who don't know I'm Crystal, Charisma's best friend and godmother to her kids. Ok, now the news everybody has been waiting for, especially for those who's been having a little wager going. Are y'all ready to know the sex of the baby?" she asked.

In unison, everybody yelled, "Yes!"

"Ok guys. Charisma and Kyron, come up here," she instructed.

Kyron and I walked up to the front of the table and stood beside Crystal. She handed us a knife so that we could cut the cake that sat before us.

"Are you guys ready? On the count of three cut into the cake… 1, 2, 3!" she yelled. Kyron and I cut into the cake I quickly looked to see if the inside was pink or blue.

"What the hell it ain't no color?" Kyron quizzed.

The sizzling of food could be heard, so we both looked up, and a server was carrying a tray that had pink smoke coming from it,

"It's a GIRL!" Crystal shouted.

Kyron kissed me on the cheek and hugged me. Everybody was hollering their told you so's and give me my money. Kyron stood up and grabbed the microphone from Crystal

"Charisma, I just want to say thank you for blessing me with a baby girl. God knows I wanted a girl. You know I accept KJ as my own son, so I didn't need another. Baby, I'm glad we still manage to make it this far through everything that we have been through. Our secrets, our memories, and all the things we have did. I really want to create more of everything with you and spend the rest of my life with you. You've been asking me all night why I kept drinking. I was nervous, baby. I want to make it official. Charisma, will you marry me?" Kyron asked.

Everybody started clapping and cheering, and I shook my head yes. I couldn't be happier. The night turned out to be beautiful. We ate, laughed, and talked and was already making plans for the baby shower. I was so tired and ready to head home. My bed was calling my name.

When we got home, I slowly dragged myself upstairs to the bedroom. I walked in the closet and started taking my clothes off, and I then went and laid across the bed in my bra and panties. Kyron came in and walked over to the bed. He took and rubbed his hand across my stomach and kissed it.

"My fat mama tired?"

"Yes lawd, I'm past tired."

"I want to get married before the baby is born. I didn't know how you felt about it because most females want to have these big huge ass weddings. What you think about that?" Kyron asked.

"Honestly, I don't want a huge wedding. You know I don't really have any family. We can do a little small wedding with me, you, Crystal and Cam. Then have our wedding reception and baby shower together," I said.

"The shit sounds like a plan to me," Kyron said. We continued talking about the wedding and baby until we both ended up dozing off. Finally, everything was coming together.

Chapter 16

Here Comes Baby!

"Push, Charisma, push!" the doctor coached. I had been in labor for forty-two hours and now was finally pushing.

"Uggggh!" I screamed.

"C'mon baby, I see the head!" Kyron yelled.

"Shut up, Kyron!" I screamed.

"One more push Charisma, make it a big one," the doctor said. I pushed with all my might until I heard the cries of my baby girl.

"Baby, she's beautiful and got a head full of hair," Kyron said. I threw my head back on my pillow and closed my eyes for a second until I felt them laying her on my chest.

"Look, baby. Here's our sweet baby girl." I held the most precious fat little girl. She had them gray eyes like her daddy. There was no doubt this was Kyron's baby with them eyes.

"Destiny, I want to name her Destiny," I told Kyron.

"I love that, baby," Kyron said.

Crystal and one of her guy friends Clarence came up to the hospital to see the baby and me. You're probably wondering what happened to Cam. Well, he found out about her ass and all she was doing. When I was seven months pregnant with Destiny, Kyron and I had a small elopement ceremony at the Belmont Mansion. Cam and

Crystal were our witnesses, so we thought everything was fine with them, but that day shit hit the fan after our wedding. We had left the mansion and headed to Crystal's for a little dinner. Well, during dinner, we had an unexpected dinner guest. It was Clarence, and he wasn't too happy to see Cam and Crystal together, and he told Cam everything. So, since that day Cam had been on a fuck bitch's spree.

***

Visiting hours were over, and I sent Destiny to the nursery, I was finally about to get some rest. My pain medicine was kicking in. Kyron had left to go drop KJ off at his granny's and said he would be back before I wake in the morning. I was feeling great I was slipping off into la la land.

The fog that surrounded me made it hard to see, but I could tell I was at my favorite park. I had a trail that I loved to walk, and the flowers and the trees along it made it so pretty. As I neared the park bench, I saw Kase sitting there.

"Kase," I whispered.

"Hey Charisma, sit down we need to talk," he demanded.

"Kase, I really miss you, and KJ does too."

"I know y'all do. I watch y'all every day. I see you're finally happy. You're married and just had a new baby, but there's a storm ahead. You will be challenged, and the trust you have for someone will be ruined. If I were still alive, you wouldn't have to go through any of this because our love was gone bring us together. You're going to

have to rely on a person that you least expect to see you through this storm, but only you will know what to do from there. I promise the decision you make will be the beginning of something new for you and your family," he said.

"Kase, I'm confused. What are you trying to tell me?" I asked starting to panic. Kase stood up, grabbed my hand, and kissed it.

"I told you everything that I could tell you, but trust me you can ride this storm out. I love you, Charisma," Kase said while walking off into the sunset till her disappeared.

I jumped up out of my sleep to a quiet knock on the door. These fucking meds had me tripping. The door opened, and Cam peeped his head in.

"Sup, girl," he said, walking into the room.

"How did you get in here? Visiting hours are over."

"Let's just say I had to tell the night nurse, I just drove over three hundred miles to see my goddaughter, and I gave her a nice little tip," Cam said.

"What's wrong?" he asked.

"I just had the strangest dream," I told Cam about my dream and told him what Kase said.

"That's some deep shit, and I wouldn't sleep on it. Take it as a sign. I believe in all that type shit. I stopped by and seen Destiny. She's a doll. Kyron and I gone have to double up on guns," Cam said.

"If I may ask Cam, it's after midnight why you just now coming up here?" I asked.

Cam laughed.

"Because I knew if I came up here, you would wake up and talk to me. You know I barely sleep," he said. He went on to tell me how the Crystal situation really fucked him up because he felt something for her. He thought she was the next best thing to me. We talked till about three in the morning. Destiny had come in for a feeding, and he sat there while I fed her. I sent her back to the nursery and Cam decided he would leave.

Before Cam walked out the door, he turned to me and said, "I really wish Destiny would have been mine," then he left.

Cam left me pondering our whole conversation. We never really talked like that since the first night we shared together in the hotel. Then the dream I had with Kase and what he said to me. I couldn't shake these emotions. All I knew for now that at this current moment, I was happy. I was married and had the perfect family— a son and now a daughter. Things just couldn't seem to get worse. Nope, not right now. Whenever that storm did decide to hit, it wasn't shit I wasn't prepared for.

Chapter 17

One Year Later

Today was Destiny's first birthday, and I was so excited for her birthday party. Things with my family couldn't have been better. Everyone was healthy and happy. I don't know what storm Kase was talking about, but me and mine were good. I had invested in a new male best friend, yes male, and his name was Cam. With him being Destiny's godfather, you couldn't pay him to be out of the picture. I talked to him more about my problems than I did Crystal. Since she got with Clarence, she had drastically changed. She stopped working at the shop, and I saw she was trying to cover up a black eye at one point. I tried reaching out to her, but she didn't want to hear anything I had to say. I still love her. I just hope she knows that I'm here if she ever needs me. She will forever be my friend.

Cupcakes by Mo had made Destiny's cake, and I had just picked it up. Cam had taken Destiny shopping. Don't ask me why he was taking a one-year-old shopping like she could pick out what she wanted, but he hated when I told him not to do something if it was in regards to Destiny. After getting the cake out the car, I walked up on the porch, and I noticed a present on the porch. Ringing the doorbell because I was holding the cake and couldn't unlock the door, Kyron came to the door.

"Oh hey baby, let me get that," he said, taking the cake out of my hands.

I turned around and picked the present up off the porch. I looked to see if it had a name on it, it just said *To Bell Family.* I walked into the kitchen.

"What's that baby?" Kyron asked, kissing me on the cheek.

"I don't know, baby. It was on the porch. Probably from somebody who couldn't make it to the party."

"That's weird. Why didn't they just didn't ring the doorbell."

"I don't know, but I don't have time to worry about it, I got to get dress. Cam should be back with Destiny in a few," I said, rushing upstairs.

While I was in the shower, I told myself that when I went back downstairs, I was gone open that box. I continue to lather my body, and then I got a bad feeling in the pit of my stomach. Something wasn't right, and I felt it. Being a mother, my mind drifted to my kids. I grabbed a towel and hopped out of the shower fast as hell and called Cam. He answered the phone on the first ring.

"We downstairs, girl."

"Oh ok I had a bad feeling, and I was just trying to check on Destiny. I'll be down in a minute," I said. I hung up the phone and started to put my clothes on. After I got dressed, I headed downstairs.

"Hey, fat mama," I cooed to Destiny as I walked into the kitchen.

"Cam, goodness, what's with all the bags?" I asked, looking in the bags.

"You know how I do," he said. I shook my head knowing not to question it.

"What's this?" Cam said pointing to the present that I had brought in earlier.

"Aw yeah, I said I was gone open it when I got done, it was sitting on the porch when I came back with the cake," I said, picking up the box. I tore the paper off the box.

"Who's it from?" Cam asked.

"It didn't say," I replied, using a knife to cut the tape off and open the box. It was a letter and some pictures.

Hey, Ms. Charisma,

Well, should I say, Mrs. Bell? I figured you should know the things that are happening around you since you practically living a lie. Just look at the pictures enclosed. They say a picture is worth a thousand words. Hahaha, make sure you read the captions on the back of the pictures.

Sincerely, an old friend

Placing the letter down, I reached into the box and removed some pictures. The first picture was a picture of a little girl. I felt myself getting hot and the steam rising off the back of my neck. I turned the picture over to read the caption. It read: *Kyla age 2.* I looked at the second picture, which was of a little girl and her daddy it read *Kyla and Daddy.* The third picture was a picture of a pregnant female holding her pregnant belly. It read: *Me currently six months pregnant.* I closed my eyes, and Cam looked at me.

"What the hell is all that?" he asked reading the letter and then picking up the pictures.

"Yo, this little girl looks just like Destiny, wait a minute. Nah, this can't be what I think it is," Cam said, looking at me. My eyes were bloodshot red, and I was ready to kill.

Kyron came walking in the kitchen, and all I saw was red.

"Wassup with y'all, why everybody so quiet?" he asked. Cam slid the pictures towards Kyron.

"Who the fuck is Kyla?" I whispered. Kyron looked at the pictures, and he shook his head in defeat.

"WHO THE FUCK IS KYLA?" I yelled. Kyron held his head down.

"WHAT NOW MOTHERFUCKER YOU CAN'T FUCKING SPEAK, NIGGA, YOU GOT A FUCKING TWO-YEAR-OLD AND ONE ON THE WAY. YOU BEEN FUCKING THE ENEMY THE WHOLE DAMN TIME. YOU BEEN FUCKING BRIA, KYRON?" I yelled throwing a glass at him barely missing his face. Kyron ducked

"It's not what you think, Charisma. Let me explain," he pleaded.

"Let you explain, how the fuck you gone explain a two-year-old who got them damn gray ass eyes like you and Destiny? Hell, I almost thought it was Destiny when I was looking at the picture, plus the bitch is pregnant now. You know what. I need you to get the fuck out right now. I'm not finna deal with this now because I'm liable to kill your ass," I blew out while pacing the floor.

"But it's Destiny's birthday," he said.

"You wasn't thinking about Destiny when you were fucking Bria, so you go play daddy to your other kids and get the fuck out!" I spat.

Kyron looked at me like he wasn't about to leave. Looking over at the knife set, I grabbed the biggest one and tried charging him.

"Whoa, Charisma put the knife down," Cam said, grabbing me.

"I'm leaving," Kyron said, walking out the house.

Cam turned to me and held me while I cried out in rage.

"Charisma, you got to be strong and not get to upset, I know you're angry, but think about your kids. They need you," he said.

"He was right, Cam," I cried.

"Who was right?" Cam asked.

"Kase, he told me a storm was coming into my life," I cried. Cam held me tighter. Whatever was brewing behind this storm, I was about to ride it out.

Chapter 18
Kyron

A nigga had no idea this would ever happen. I truly loved Charisma, but I just couldn't shake Bria. I loved all my children with all my heart and was thankful for Bria giving me kids, but at this very moment, I was ready to kill her ass. I drove to Bria's house on a rampage. This hoe was going to make me choke her ass out. I couldn't believe that she did this shit on my daughter birthday.

I pulled up to her house and hopped out the car using my key to enter the house.

"Bria!" I called out. Bria came from the back wearing this evil grin on her face like she knew exactly what she had done.

Yes, sir?" she flashed an evil smile. I got up in her face.

"Why in the fuck would you do this to me? On my daughter's birthday at that. You don't want for anything. I make sure you and my daughter are straight, I'm at every doctor's appointment, and I'm here when you need me. What else do you want from me?" I yelled.

Bria sucked her teeth.

"Kyron, you need to be with me, that's why. I love you. Why can't you see that?" Bria whined.

"Look, Bria. You know why this can't happen. I am a married man, and I love my wife. It's bad enough that I continued this thing with you. You're not stable, and you really need to get some help before I take my kids away from you."

"Why, so you and that bitch Charisma can raise my girls? I would kill myself and the girls before I let that bitch raise my kids. You won't be married for long. I know Charisma. She's not gone forgive you that easy." Bria chuckled and laughed evilly.

***

Bria was right that day. Charisma hit my ass with divorce papers within two weeks. I honestly was shocked, but I knew I had really hurt her to the core. It's been months, and she still won't talk to me. Cam has been bringing KJ and Destiny to see me so that I could spend time with them. I give her that she does allow me to see the kids.

Charisma

Kyron finally decided to give me my divorce. I don't know what made him think we could work this out. I don't have anything to say to him now either. Cam has been wonderful through this whole process, and I do mean wonderful. I got a feeling that Cam's feelings for me are a little more then what I feel for him now. It's too soon to be rushing into anything with anyone right now. He's very helpful with the kids and to my bedroom needs. I walked out of the bathroom and tiptoed back to Cam's bed trying not to wake him.

"Charisma, what are you doing?" Cam stirred in his sleep. I sat on the bed.

"Nothing about to head home," I said. Cam turned to face me.

"Why you never stay the night? You be treating a nigga like a booty call," Cam said.

Letting out a huge sigh, I ran my hands through my hair.

"Cam, I'm just trying not to get any feelings attached. Everything that has been going on is a little much for me right now," I said, trying not to sound completely cold.

Cam sat up in the bed and looked me dead in my eyes like he wasn't comprehending what I said.

"So you've really just been using me for sex? It sounds to me somebody named Cha Cha is making her return. How the hell we go from best friends to fuck friends? Charisma I'm here, and I've been here through everything you've been through. Not once have I judged you or left you out to dry. I love your kids as if they were my own. Now all of a sudden you're acting brand new because the last nigga hurt you. You were so caught up about that dream you had about Kase, but I guess you forgot about the rest? I swear I don't even want to say this shit, but I've been holding it in. I fucking love you and want to be with you. I don't know why you choose now to shut me out and not see it for what's it worth," Cam said.

I put my hands on my head because I was getting a headache, and this was all too much. I cared for Cam, but my heart was just torn to pieces.

"Look, Cam. I appreciate everything, but us being together right now just can't happen."

Easing out of Cam's bed, I started putting my clothes on. The vibe in the room was completely different now. As I was about to walk out the door, I turned back around to look at Cam. Our eyes met, and he did the unexpected. He turned his back on me.

I went back and forth with myself on whether to pick KJ and Destiny up from KJ's granny or not. I needed time to think, so I opted to pick them up in the morning. While sitting in the car, I lit the blunt I had sitting in my ashtray and turned the music up vibing along to Jodeci's "Freek'n You". That blunt took me to a different level, and I wanted to have a few drinks, so I headed to Brugada's and indulged in some drinks and hookah since I had a few friends that worked there. I walked straight to the bar and ordered an 8-liquor ass kicker.

Sitting at the bar enjoying my drink and moving to the music, I felt a tap on the shoulder.

"Well damn, if it isn't Cha Cha!" the guy yelled over the loud music. I turned around and locked eyes with Taye.

"Damn, it's been a minute. I see you still looking good," I flirted. I knew it was the liquor talking.

"I was just about to say the same thing about you," Taye said, eyeing me up and down.

"I heard you had gotten married. Ion see no ring on your finger though."

"That's because I'm divorced now," I said, sipping from my drink. Taye and I spent the rest of the night catching up.

**

All I could hear was ringing. My phone was ringing off the hook. I stirred and removed my head from underneath the cover, grabbing the phone.

"Hello," I answered groggily.

"Girl, if you don't get your ass up and come and get these kids. I am going to Bingo, and it's damn near noon!" KJ's granny yelled in the phone.

"Oh shit, Ms. Patty, I'm on the way," I panicked. You can hear Ms. Patty still cussing in the background.

Climbing out the bed, I noticed a body in bed me. Pulling the covers back I was shocked to see Taye. What in the fuck happened last night? I gave Taye a push.

"Taye, get up. I got to go get my kids." Both of us were scrambling around getting dress, and the news stopped me in my feet.

"Reporting live on the scene where they believe a woman drove her car into the Cumberland River last night. Authorities and

rescue team has been out all night on this very sad scene. The woman appeared to be pregnant and had a two-year-old little girl in the car with her as well. Both bodies have been recovered from the river. The victims appear to be that of twenty-six-year-old Bria Adam's and two-year-old Kyla Bell. We will keep you updated more on the scene," said the news reporter.

Placing my hands to my mouth, I let out a loud gasp, "Oh my god!"

Chapter 19

Kyron

I sat here in the dark house. I haven't showered or ate anything for two days. Ever since I got the news about Bria and my daughters, I had been in a terrible depressive state. I never imagined my whole life falling apart within a year. There was a knock at the door, but I just sat there paying it no attention. Whoever it was wasn't letting up and kept knocking.

"Kyron," I heard the familiar voice say.

I got up from the couch, walked over to the door, and looked out the peephole. Rubbing my eyes and making sure that I wasn't tripping, I looked again before opening the door. I stood there looking at the familiar face that I missed so much.

"Um hi," Charisma said.

"Hey," I mumbled.

"May I come in?" she asked. I moved over letting Charisma in the house.

Charisma

I looked around, and the stench of the place was enough to make me sick to the stomach. I sat my purse on the counter and turned to look at Kyron.

"Kyron, I'm sorry for your loss. I know Bria and I didn't like each other, but what she did was terrible. I don't know what it feels like to lose a child, well children for that matter. However, you still have Destiny here that you must be strong for and giving up is not an option. Not if my life depends on it. I will not let you tear yourself down or blame yourself for this," I told him.

"Go take a shower and clean yourself up. Please for me."

I didn't know if he would listen, but when he walked off, I smiled. Looking around, the place was a mess, so I started to pick a few things. While Kyron was in the shower, I decided to fix him something to eat. I'm sure he hasn't eaten in days. While breakfast was cooking, I continued to clean the kitchen and get it back to looking like someone lived here.

Shortly after, Kyron entered the kitchen wearing a pair of basketball shorts and wifebeater. He had his dreads pulled up in a ponytail on his head. He looked around at the spotless house and smiled. I had the table decked out with pancakes, turkey bacon, cheese eggs, and fresh fruit. I was going to take the trash out, but that shit was far as hell.

"Why in the hell is the dumpster in these condo's so damn far away?"

"You didn't have to do all this," Kyron said.

"Yes, I did. It even smells better in here, and you even smell better. I know we haven't been on good terms, but I wasn't gone let you go through this all this alone," I said.

Kyron sat down at the table and smashed his breakfast. I knew he missed my cooking.

"I take it you haven't cleaned this house for longer than two days dude. This shit was a mess," I voiced. Kyron chuckled.

"A nigga's been down for too long. I never got to tell you I was sorry for what I did," Kyron said.

The awkwardness caused me to shift in my seat because we have yet to talk about us.

"I just got what I deserved I guess," I admitted.

"Nobody deserves that, Charisma. I can't even give you a valid reason as to why I even did it, but I'm truly sorry," he apologized.

"I got payback for everything I did to you, and now I feel I will never love again. That shit hurt me to my soul," I added.

Kyron removed my shoes and started massaging my feet. I closed my eyes and laid my head back on the couch. Kyron put my foot down and leaned in and kissed Charisma me on the neck.

"No stop, Kyron. We are not about to do this," I said, pushing Kyron away from me.

"Please Charisma, I need this right now, and I need you all of you," he pleaded.

I knew he was vulnerable, and I guess one last time wouldn't hurt. Kyron lifted me and took me to the bedroom and laid me down on the bed where he satisfied his craving that he missed so much. I was his safe haven, and I wasn't sure why I even allowed this to happen. I had no intentions of coming over here to sleep with him. I just wanted to console him and make sure he gets through this loss. I was fucking weak. The sex was good, but it couldn't happen again. My heart just couldn't open back up to him.

Silence had taken over me. I just wanted to get the hell out of dodge. I got dressed so fast so that I could leave.

"Do you want me to bring Destiny over here so you can have some entertainment and maybe take your mind off some things?" I asked Kyron.

"Yeah, I would love that you can bring her a bag so that she can stay a couple of days. You think KJ would want to come to?" he asked.

"I can see. You know he still a little upset with you," I admitted.

"Yeah, he always a little distant with me unless Cam's around," he said. The mentioning of Cam's name made me uncomfortable as hell.

"Well, I'll call you when I'm headed back this way," I said and walked out the door.

***

A few days had passed, and Cam told me to bring KJ to the shop so that he could get a haircut. When I pulled up to the shop, I got out and took KJ in.

"Hey y'all!" I spoke to everybody in the shop.

"Where's Cam?" I asked.

"He's back in the office," another barber answered. I walked back towards the office and knocked on the door.

"Come in," he called out.

Peeking inside, I voiced, "Hey, KJ is out there. Who's gone cut his hair?" I asked.

"Come in. We need to talk," Cam demanded.

"What's wrong?" I asked, sitting down across from him.

"I wanted to be the first to tell you that I'm going back to Atlanta for a minute," he spoke.

"What's a minute? A weekend, a week?" I questioned. The mere mention of leaving made me weak.

"I don't know. It may be longer than that. I need to go home for a while. Ain't shit here," Cam said coldly, looking at me with a blank face.

All I could do was nod my head and suck my teeth because I was pissed off. I'm not gone lie and say it didn't bother me. I told him I didn't want a relationship, but I secretly loved Cam. I just couldn't bring myself to be with him.

"What you mean ain't shit here? What about me and the kids?" I yelled, spilling out my emotions.

"What about you? My god kids are gone be straight whether I'm here or California. You, on the other hand, I don't owe you anything. I tried to be with you, but you pushed me off to go run in the arms of another nigga. Well niggas, excuse me." Cam chuckled.

My face was screwed up showing confusion.

"You know the barbershop talks and so does Kyron. Ion even know that nigga Taye but him and Kyron were chopping it up on some random shit, and somehow your name came up. You need to get your shit together. I'll drop KJ off when I'm done with him," Cam said as he walked out the office, leaving me sitting there looking stupid.

Chapter 20

Four Months Later

I couldn't believe Cam actually left and took his ass back to Atlanta, stubborn ass. He would FaceTime the kids all the time and one time he came up and took them back to Atlanta to take them to Six Flags, but he will not speak to me about anything unless it's regarding the kids. It's crazy how you really don't miss somebody until their gone. Here I was in love with a man who I hurt, and he didn't want anything to do with me.

It was a pretty September day, and I was walking into the medical plaza with not a care in the world. Once I stepped on the elevator, I pressed the 5 for the fifth floor. When I got off and turned the corner, I ran into Kyron. I looked around frantically.

"What you doing here?" I asked.

"I'm leaving from seeing my doctor," he answered.

"Your doctor? When did your ass start going to the doctor?" I asked.

"Yes, my doctor. A nigga has been having chest pains and shit, and they sent me to a heart specialist."

"Is everything cool?" I asked.

"Yeah, I'm good. What are you doing here?"

"Routine checkup, nothing major," I lied.

"Aw ok, you need me to get Destiny from daycare?" he asked.

"You can if you want."

"Aite then," he said, walking off. I waited until he got on the elevator and headed to my doctor's office.

Walking into the office, I checked in for my appointment, took my seat, and waited until my name was called. The nervous feeling in the pit of my stomach mixed in with the queasiness was not a good feeling.

"Ms. Johnson!" the nurse called my name. I got up and followed the nurse in the back.

"Ok step up here and let's get your weight," she said. I stood on the scale.

"Ok, can I get you to give me a urine sample, and I'll be waiting on you in the next room." I took the specimen cup and went into the bathroom.

I came back out of the bathroom and handed her the cup and sat down. "Do you have any questions or concerns for the doctor?" the nurse asked.

"No, ma'am," I answered.

"Ok the doctor will be with your shortly," the nurse said before leaving out the room.

I sat patiently in the room looking around at all the things that were in the room. Finally, I heard a knock on the door and in walked the doctor.

"Ms. Johnson, how you feeling?" she asked.

"I actually feel great," I said.

"You should you have gained some weight this month instead of losing. That means you finally on the right track with this baby. Every pregnancy is different. A lot of women lose weight and gain it right back. I was concerned at first, especially with you being four months and that belly is barely showing. I need for you to keep eating the things I told you and stay stress-free as possible, and we will have you picking up weight in no time," she insisted.

"Yes, ma'am."

Yes, I'm pregnant, and it is Cam's baby. My ass had gotten pregnant, and I didn't even know until after he had already left for Atlanta. Nobody knows I'm pregnant. I'd been losing weight, so I was barely showing like the doctor said. I planned on telling Cam when the time was right. I gathered my things and headed out of the doctor's office. When I walked into the hall, Kyron was standing there, scaring the fuck out of me.

"Routine checkup, huh?" he asked.

"Why in the hell are you standing around here watching folks?"

"Are you pregnant, Charisma?" he asked. I sighed and rolled my eyes.

"That's none of your business," I said and turned to walk off. Kyron grabbed my arm.

"You're pregnant, ain't you?" he asked again.

"Yes, now leave me alone," I said, walking off again.

"Hold up, is it mine?"

"No, Kyron, it is not yours," I said, getting aggravated by the minute. He stood there looking hurt.

"Well who's baby is it?" he asked. Lord knows I didn't want to hurt him, but if his ass hadn't gone back talking shit about what we had going on, Cam's ass would be here and not in Atlanta.

"Cam's," I said and kept walking to the elevator. Once in the elevator, I started beating myself up because I knew he was going to go and tell Cam this shit. *Fuck!*

I headed to pick KJ and Destiny up from school and daycare. Kyron was pissed, so I guess he forgot to pick up Destiny. The kids and I headed home and settled into our normal routine. The kids were in their rooms playing, and I was in the kitchen fixing us something for dinner. My FaceTime started ringing, and I saw it was Cam. *Oh my god.* I didn't answer, and he called right back.

"KJ, come get the phone. It's Cam!" I yelled. KJ came running in the kitchen and answered the phone.

"Sup, Cam!" he yelled all hyped up.

"What up fat head, where's your ma at? I need to talk to her," he said. I shook my head no at KJ. I didn't want the phone.

"Right here," KJ said, turning the phone around on me. I grabbed the phone.

"KJ, go back in there and see what Destiny is doing!" I spat. I turned the phone back on me and looked at Cam. *Damn, he was fine as hell.*

"So, tell me why I get a phone call from your baby daddy talking out the side of his fucking neck telling me you pregnant and shit. What's that all about?" Cam asked.

"I am pregnant." I sighed. Cam rubbed his head.

"Is it mine?" he asked.

"Yes," I replied.

"Charisma, why the fuck do you keep playing with me?" he said angrily.

Silence.

"You know what. I got to tie up some loose ends here, and I'll be back in Nashville tonight, so have your ass up!" he spat and ended the call.

I was scared as hell, and I ain't going to lie. I wanted to call Kyron up and cuss his hating ass out, but what was done was done, and now it is what it is.

***

It was close to midnight, and I was on edge waiting on Cam to get here. I had cleaned the entire house and took me a nice bubble bath and rubbed my body down. I wasn't trying to get cute, but I didn't want him to see me looking bad either. I put on some yoga pants and a matching sports bra so he could see what tiny bump I had. Maybe that will calm him down a little bit. I pulled my hair up in a bun. That's when the doorbell rang.

Looking through the peephole, seeing him made my insides all warm and fuzzy. I opened the door. Jesus, I almost fainted. Cam stood there in a Polo jogger, his beard was freshly trimmed, and he had his hat down low over his eyes. He looked up, and we locked eyes. I smiled slightly. He looked down at my little tummy, walked in the door, and grabbed me. We hugged for what felt like an eternity.

"I swear to God if you ever play with my heart like you did before Charisma, I will leave your ass for good."

"I promise I won't, Cam. I love you so much. I always have, I was just scared. Can I have my best friend back?" I asked.

"You can have that and so much more. Girl, you finna be my wife. I told you a long time ago when you were pregnant with Destiny. I was gone marry the mother of my child," he said. We walked into the living room and sat down on the couch.

"Why you so small though, baby?" he asked.

"Stress I guess, and the doctor said I was getting better though because I had gained some weight."

"Well, we gone stay on that. Daddy's home so no more stress and worries," he said. I looked at Cam.

"What did Kyron say, was he mad at you? He won't talk to me." I laughed.

"He was pretty upset. I tried telling him how our friendship just escalated after he left. He went all the way back talking bout we been fucking since we had that threesome, I was saying to myself we were fucking before then. I couldn't tell him anything that he would believe. He had his mindset and said fuck me."

"I hate that, what about the businesses?"

"Money is gone be made regardless. Both our names are on them businesses. He can either buy out or shut up and keep making money," he said. We continued to talk until we dozed off on the couch.

I saw Kase standing near the light

"You got it Charisma. I thought I had lost you for a minute. He is the one to change your life and family for the better. Enjoy your life and just remember that I'm always watching you. I love you," Kase said, and he walked off into the sunset in my dreams.

Epilogue

Eight Months Later

Today was the day I finally get to marry the man of my dreams. I'd been getting cold feet. I ain't gone lie. However, I knew he was the man for me, plus Kase told me so. I stood on the other side of the church door waiting to walk down this aisle to my man. Finally, the doors of the church open and Jesse Powell's "You" started playing on the speakers.

Destiny and KJ walked down the aisle first as flower girl and ring bearer. I looked up at the front of the church, and there stood my handsome ass husband to be. I looked over to my bridesmaids, and Crystal was holding my son Cameron Jr. Yes, Crystal. She came back around a couple of months ago after she finally left Clarence's abusive ass. I had my best friend back, and I was so happy about that. It was now my turn to walk down the aisle.

Zoned out and on a high that I couldn't describe, I walked down the aisle to meet my husband. It wasn't a dry eye in the house. Even Cam eyes were glossy as hell. To see him tear up did something to me. Besides the birth of our son, I had never seen him cry. When it came time to do our vows, and it was my turn, I looked Cam in his eyes.

"Cam…" I started.

"WAIT!!!" a voice said, busting into the church. Everyone turned around and in walked Kyron.

"What the fuck is this shit?" Cam stormed off walking down to meet him halfway.

"You done lost your damn mind nigga walking up in here interrupting our wedding," Cam said to Kyron.

"Charisma, please hear me out?" Kyron said out of breath.

"Kyron, you need to leave," I said.

"No, please just listen," he pleaded. Cam was starting to get pissed by the minute until Kyron started talking

"Charisma, you deserve to be happy. I just wanted to give y'all my blessing. Charisma, I'm sorry for bringing you so much pain. I hope you can find it your heart to forgive me one day. Cam, I know you have been here through everything that happened within our lives, and one thing remains, you never changed. I see your love for Charisma and the kids. If anything, I want someone who I know my daughter loves and will be happy with. That's all y'all, and I'm sorry I interrupted this very important day, but I had to get that off my chest," Kyron said. Cam dapped Kyron and hugged him.

"Thanks, man," he said.

"Thank you, Kyron." I smiled.

Kyron turned to walked out of the church, and when he was midway to the door, he collapsed.

"Daddy!" Destiny screamed running towards Kyron. Cam ran to check on Kyron, and a few other folks gathered around.

"Somebody call an ambulance!" Cam yelled. Kyron's pulse was getting weaker and weaker.

"Don't worry about me, go finish getting married," Kyron faintly said.

"What?" Cam asked.

"Go finish marrying her. She doesn't need to wait any longer," he said before closing his eyes. Cam looked at everyone gathered around.

"Go ahead. The ambulance is on the way. He's gone," a guest of the wedding said.

"We got it covered," they said. Cam turned and walked back down the aisle towards Charisma, and he grabbed her hand.

"He's gone, but he said to finish the wedding," Cam said.

"What?" I screamed out in shock.

"He said to finish the wedding. Those were literally his last words," Cam said, looking at the pastor and consoling me. The pastor did what he was told and finished the wedding.

This will literally be a day we all would never forget. Kyron died from hypertrophic cardiomyopathy. I guess that explains why I'd seen him at the heart doctor a while back.

Since then life has been smooth sailing. Cam, the kids, and I were enjoying our family life. We had moved into an even bigger house. Cam said it was because he wanted more kids, but I wasn't about to have any more kids for a hot minute. We were outside enjoying the pool, and I was enjoying lying in the sun, I had dozed off for a split second, and what I saw made me smile even more. Kase and Kyron were laughing and talking all while looking at me.

"Live it up, Charisma. You deserve it," Kase said.

"Forever and always," said Kyron.

They walked off into the sunset, and I woke up and took in my surroundings. Cam came running towards me and picked me up. He was about to throw me in the pool, and I was kicking and screaming for him to put me down.

"Stop playing put me down, Cam!" I yelled. He threw me into the pool laughing, and the kids were laughing right along with him.

"Oh my god, Cam, you play too much. Ugh, I hate you," I yelled. He jumped in the pool and kissed me.

"But I love you, girl." He smiled, causing me to laugh. I let our lips touch and savored the effects my husband had on me.

The End

Letter from the author

Thank you for reading, and I hoped you enjoyed *Me vs. Me: Life of Deceit*. I have another goody in store for you. Turn the page and enjoy another novella, which is also a rerelease of *Deception: City of Lies*. Both books deal with the outcome of one's lies and how detrimental the outcome can be.

Deception

Kyeate

Chapter 1

Daryll

Deception: the act of hiding the truth

Nashville, TN it's a big city but amazingly small when things and people run together. I'm that suave brother who had the streets on lock in the 80s and 90s. I was the biggest dealer in the city. I'm Daryll "Kingpin" Miles. You name it, and I had it all— women, houses, cars, taking trips. Having my share of women whom to this day has caused havoc in my life, I lucked up and only had two sons, Darius and Darnell. They grew up on opposite sides of the track, not knowing one another. I loved my boys, but I did this purposely so that when I die, they wouldn't have a care in the world. Now that I'm dying and on my death bed, it's time I come clean to my sons to let them know about each other.

Darius

I'm Darius Miles, twenty-four years young and son of Daryll Miles. You can say I'm just like my pops, I took over the drug business, and now I run the city. I'm well respected here in Nashville. I had received a call from my pops asking me to stop by the hospital today because we needed to talk. I had been spending as much time with my old man because his time was near. My pops had been battling prostate cancer for a minute now, and it's starting to take its toll on him. I've been staying busy to keep my mind off the situation. It's hard being the only child because it seems like the weight of the world is on my shoulders at times. I don't know what it is that pops want to talk about, but whatever it was sounded urgent.

Darnell

"Yes dad, I'll be there once I get finished with this last meeting," I said into the phone.

"I love you, son."

"I love you too," I replied and hung up the phone. I touched the page button.

"Yes, boss?" the delicate voice came through the speaker.

"Clear my schedule for the rest of the day, Ebony. I have a family emergency."

"Yes sir, Mr. Taylor," Ebony answered.

Leaning back in my chair I looked around my office, thinking about how great a life I had made for myself with the help of my father. All the plaques hanging around were even better. At twenty-six years old, I ran the biggest and most popular law firm in Nashville, Taylor & Miles. I wasn't aware of what exactly my father wanted to talk about today, but he demanded my presence. I hope everything is ok.

A knocked at the door, brought me out of my thoughts.

"Come in," I called out.

Ebony walked into the office and closed the door. She was a sight to see. She sauntered towards me and stood behind my chair and rubbed my shoulders.

"Is everything ok, baby? What's the family emergency?" she asked.

"I don't even know myself. My dad wants me to come to the hospital as soon as I'm done." I sighed. Ebony walked around the chair and took a seat in my lap.

"Well, I sure hope everything is alright," Ebony said and planted a kiss on my lips.

I returned the favor and kissed Ebony back. Her soft lips and warm tongue were causing me to brick up in my pants. I knew I had no business fooling around with Ebony. She was an intern here at my firm, but she put it on so thick that a man couldn't resist.

Ebony

I'm Ebony Rose, yes, that's my real name. I've been interning here at Taylor & Miles for six months. I'm almost done with my intern, but I've already got a job lined up thanks to my boo Darnell. Darnell and I been dating for about four months. At first, he came off as stuck up I guess because he is a lawyer, but the man is hood. I guess you can't judge a book by its cover. Folks used to think the same about me as if I couldn't make something out of myself because I was raised in James Cayce projects. Darnell and I had so much in common that it was ridiculous. I guess that's why we clicked.

Darius

I pulled up at the hospital ready to see my dad. Hopping out, I handed valet the keys to my truck.

"Take care of my shit," I told the valet attendant.

My demeanor was that of a boss and nothing less. I didn't take no shit, so strangers often feared me. My drip was on point, and I took pride in my shit. It was mandatory that I looked like the money I made. I was rocking some all black Balmain Jeans and a white and black Balmain shirt, with a diamond encrusted gold chain that had my initials DM on it that my father gave me— simple but expensive taste for a hood nigga. Glancing down at my ringing phone, I saw it was Jazmine.

"You gone have to wait, shorty," I said while pressing ignore on the phone. I made my way up the third floor and walked into my father's room the room where he laid watching television.

"Pops!" I called out with a little bit more excitement than usual. The love I had for my father was like no other. My dad was like my best friend. My father looked up and seen me.

"Oh, hey boy," he smiled. I walked over to the bed and gave my dad a peck on his forehead.

"How are you feeling?"

"I'm feeling as good as I can for an almost dead man," he responded. I shook my head.

"Pops, I swear you are something else," I said sitting in the chair next to the bed.

"So, what's so important that you had to see me right away?" I asked. Whatever it was I could tell it was taking its toll on him. My father looked tired beyond the cancer as if he was beating himself up about something.

"Well son, there's no easy way to say this, but it's time for you to know that you have a brother," my father spoke. I leaned forward looking at my dad like he was crazy.

"What you mean I got a brother?"

"Like I said Darius, you have an older brother." He coughed.

"I'm saying did you just find out about him or something, why are you just now telling me this?" A nigga was heated.

"No son, I been in his life the whole time just like I was yours," he admitted.

The opening of his room door interrupted us. In walked Mr. Taylor, that I knew because he was my lawyer dressed to kill in a Tom Ford suit.

"Mr. Taylor, what are you doing here?" I got up to greet him with a dap. Mr. Taylor let out a deep laugh.

"Hoping that you're staying out of trouble and not needing my services again," he said.

"I've been staying away from trouble. Trouble just seems to find me." I laughed. Mr. Taylor looked at my dad.

"What's up, pops? What's with the urgent news that I had to cancel some important meetings today?" he said, causing my head to whip around fast as hell.

"Pops?" I quizzed.

"Like I was saying before you came in Darnell, I was telling Darius he has an older brother. There ain't no easy way to tell y'all, but Darius Darnell is your brother," my father announced. I stood up.

"Hold on. What's going on?" Darnell asked confused as hell like I was.

"Darnell, Darius is your brother," my father spoke again.

"I mean, why would you keep this from us? This whole time I'm thinking that I'm the only child, and I got a whole brother out here. Taylor & Miles that explains the Miles in your firm," I said looking at Darnell.

My father struggled to sit up in the bed.

"Look, this was my plan the entire time. What I look like raising two drug dealers? That's why I kept y'all separate and doing different things. Now you guys really have it made. Darius, you got all of Nashville on lock coming to you for work. Darnell, you got the legal parts covered and half of MNPD on your payroll. Together you're a force that can't be touched!" Pops emphasized.

"I know you don't expect for us to accept this news and just be all brotherly. No offense, but I don't know this nigga from a can of paint," Darnell said.

"None taken and touché, my nigga," I agreed.

Darnell and I stared each other down. I couldn't see the resemblance. I peeped his cufflinks and ring with the initials DM engraved on it.

"Why do you go by Taylor?" I blurted out, asking Darnell.

"I go by both. My name is hyphenated Taylor-Miles," Darnell said. We stood in silence for a minute.

"Look I need for y'all to come together. I've never asked for much, but I'm asking now. Once I'm gone, I will no longer be here when y'all call on me. You guys are brothers and now y'all have to have each other's back," my father responded.

"I have to digest this. I will call you later." Darnell sighed and bolted out the door.

Darnell

Of all the shit my father could've thrown my way, this shit took the cake. I drove home in a daze. I couldn't believe this news. How could he spring something on me like this? I mean I didn't mind having a brother and Darius seem like a cool dude, but this was deep. It makes me wonder just how many other secrets he had kept from us.

Chapter 2

Darius

Real shit, I didn't take the news well about Darnell, but I was gone try to make the best of it for the sake of our father. Over the last week, his health deteriorated fast, and it was touch and go for him. With my head knocking to the beat of the music, I sat here in the parking lot of Taylor & Miles just staring at the name on the building. A nigga was way too familiar with this building. The whole time it was my brother helping me out of a lot of trouble in these streets, and I didn't even know. Laughing to myself, I thought about how my father knew exactly what he was doing. I got out of the car and walked inside. It was now or never.

When I got inside, I peeped the cocoa-skinned honey sitting at the front desk. When she smiled, she gave me that flirtatious bat of the eyes and hair flip.

"Welcome to Taylor & Miles, how may I help you?"

"Yeah is Darnell in, excuse me, Mr. Taylor?"

"He's in his office, but he doesn't see anyone unless they have an appointment."

"Can you just tell him Darius is here? I'm sure he will want to see me." I said.

When she stood up from the desk and walked to Darnell's office, she put an extra twitch in her hips. I just laughed. She was laying it on thick. That pencil skirt she had on was doing her justice. Her body was banging. She wasn't gone too long before she returned.

"Mr. Taylor will see you now," she said seductively. I hit her with a wink before walking into Darnell's office.

When I walked in, Darnell was standing there waiting for me.

"Your little secretary, please tell me you smashed that because she is fine as hell?" I had to ask. Darnell chuckled and shook his head

"No sir, I like to keep it professional at all times."

"Well, a nigga might need to shoot his shot when I leave out of here then," I joked but was oh so serious.

"So, to what do I owe the pleasure of this visit, little brother? Damn that sounds crazy," Darnell said.

"I was actually stopping by to talk about just that. All bullshit aside, after thinking about it, yeah what pops did was fucked up, but like it or not we are blood. We're all we got left, and I can see the bigger picture of what dad had in mind. So, I'm willing if you're willing."

Darnell leaned back in his chair and put his hands together. I could tell he was thinking.

"I can dig it little brother, but don't think your legal fees are gone come free now," Darnell said, causing both us to bust out laughing.

Standing up, I held my hand out for my brother to shake. Darnell stood up and walked around the desk and grabbing my hand and bringing me in for a hug.

I left the office feeling good that I finally talked to my brother. So good that I decided to head home and spend a little time with my gal before I had to make my rounds. Riding through the old neighborhoods that I used to hang in as a kid, I shook my head at all the changes. The hood didn't even look the same with all the changes. What used to be the slums or the hood, was now overpopulated with million-dollar homes. Hell, I could've kept my ass in the hood instead of moving way out.

About twenty minutes later, I pulled in the driveway. One thing I loved about living away from the city was the peace. I had been living in Brentwood for about a year now. Princeton Hills was a nice subdivision. Mostly doctors, lawyers, and other big-time folks lived here.

Walking into the house, I sighed because I knew Jazmine's ass ain't did shit all day. When I entered the living room, Jazmine was sitting on the couch gossiping on the phone as usual.

"I swear that's all your ass does. A nigga comes home to try to spend some time with you, and your lips are glued to the damn phone!" I spat.

Jazmine rolled her eyes and put her hands over the phone

"For your info, this is my family on a jail call. I should be off in a minute," she whispered.

Fuck that shit. I headed upstairs to the bedroom and removed my shoes. I then walked into the connecting office and opened the safe to put my money inside. Walking back into the room, I climbed in bed. Shortly after Jazmine came prancing in the room. Jazmine was hood as hell, but she looked like a goddess. She had dark brown skin and wore her natural hair that stopped a little to the middle of her back when straightened, but I liked it when she wore her natural curls. Something about it turned me the hell on. We had known each other for about six years but only been dating for a year. She was one of them she should have remained a friend type. Our relationship just wasn't what we thought it would be. I know I wasn't happy, but she held a nigga down during rough times, so I owed her.

"How you gone say you wanted to spend time with me yet you in the bed like you finna go to sleep?" she snapped with her neck rolling and shit.

"Because I did, but now I just want to sleep. Your jail call was more important, so now I'm good."

"I swear you get on my nerves."

"Well, take your ass back to your mammy's house. You ain't got to stay here."

Jazmine's mouth dropped, and she crossed her arms.

"Yeah, that's what I thought. Your lazy ass knows if you go back there, she is gone have her hand out and make your ass do something that you never done, and that's work," I finished and rolled over.

"Why are you always starting shit, Darius?" Jazmine asked. I wasn't about to go back and forth with her ass.

Darnell

On the other side of town Ebony and I was wrapping up an intense freak session. When I came out of the bathroom, Ebony was getting dressed. A nigga was trying to cuddle and shit.

"Where you headed off to?" I asked. Ebony was retouching her makeup

"Kim and I are going to 9Bar tonight."

"I guess." I shrugged. I was a little salty. Ebony turned around.

"You want me to stay here with you and look at cases all night?" Ebony joked.

"No, you go do you. I'll have my fun this weekend, and don't try to stop me. You just make sure your ass is on time for work in the morning."

"You got jokes I see," Ebony said, grabbing her purse. She hit me with a quick peck before she left out.

Darius

When I woke up and looked at the clock, it was 9:30 p.m. I hopped up so fast and got in the shower. I slept longer than I was supposed to since I had to go check on the spots. Stepping out the shower, I wrapped my towel around my waist and brushed my teeth. While looking in the mirror, Jazmine walked by and shot my ass an evil grin, causing me to look over my shoulder at her ass.

"Is there a problem?" I questioned. She sucked her teeth and kept walking.

"I got to watch her crazy ass," I mumbled to myself.

Finishing up, I walked into the closet and grabbed me something to wear. After getting dressed, I made my way back to my office to grab some money out the safe. When I turned to walk out, Jazmine was standing in the doorway.

"Where you finna go?" she asked with an attitude.

"When you start checking for a nigga? Move girl," I said, walking around her.

"I won't be here when you get back!" she yelled.

"Well, make sure you take an Uber wherever you going and leave my car right the fuck where it's at," I told her. Her ass wasn't finna go no damn where. Hell, I took care of her ass.

Jazmine

Pissed was an understatement.

"I'm sick of this shit. I got something for that ass. I don't need him for a bitch ass thing!" I yelled.

I marched over to the window to watch him pull out the driveway. Once he pulled off, I made my way to his office. Glancing around the room until my eyes landed on his safe, I smiled and went over to the safe and looked at it, thinking twice about what I was about to do. *That nigga had better stop sleeping on me.* I put the code in that I had watched Darius several times use to open this safe, and I act like I wasn't paying attention. The safe clicked, I opened it. *Jackpot.* I grabbed all the money in the safe and made a run for the door.

Looking at my arms, I decided to put some back. Finally, I ran to the closet and grabbed the bag that I had already packed, threw the money inside, and dipped.

Ebony

We had made it to 9Bar, my girl Kim and I were sitting at a booth having drinks and smoking hookah. This scene was everything, and we were vibing to the music.

"Girl I love it here. It's nice, laid back, and the food is amazing," Kim said. I could hear her, but my eyes were fixated on the door and who had just walked in.

"Kim, that's him," I said.

"Who?" Kim asked, looking in the direction of where I was looking.

"Darius, the one that I was telling you about at work today."

"Oh yeah, he is fine girl. You better go work your magic," Kim said.

"I don't want to come off as thirsty, so I'll wait a little bit."

"I don't think you have to wait at all because bitch he is headed this way," Kim said, acting cool. Darius walked up.

"I thought that was your sexy ass," Darius said smiling, showing his pearly whites. My face got hot. I couldn't believe I was blushing.

"Cat got her tongue, but hi I'm Kim, her best friend," Kim said, greeting Darius.

"Nice to meet you, Kim. Is it ok if my boy and I chill over here with y'all? Everything is on us."

"That's fine," Kim said. Me, on the other hand, I wanted to shit my pants.

***

The night was going great. After I had a few drinks, Darius and I had been talking and getting to know each other. He wasn't big on many details about his personal life, but he did show a lot of interest in getting to know me. So, I didn't mind sharing details about me or my life.

"So, where's your nigga at? You're too beautiful to be single," Darius asked.

I didn't feel the need to tell him about my relationship with Darnell because with me being his intern it was supposed to be a secret.

"I'm single, just focusing on graduating and possibly becoming a lawyer one day."

"That means I can take you out on a date, right?" he asked.

"I don't see why not." I smiled. We exchanged numbers, and he said he had to bounce. Just like that, he was gone like a thief in the night.

Darius

Good thing I ran into Ebony, I was for sure finna put her on my team since Jazmine's ass was tripping. Speaking of which, she had texted me while inside, but I ignored it because I was entertaining Kim. When I finally opened the text from Jazmine, this hoe had sent me a picture of my fucking safe open. I could tell some money was gone out of it.

"I'm gone hurt that bitch," I seethed, calling Jazmine's phone. The bitch ain't answer. Next, I dialed my right hand man

"Aye bruh, I need you to make rounds for me. This bitch done hit my safe and is not answering the fucking phone," I told my homie, Clint.

"I got you. I'm on it now," Clint said and hung up the phone.

I did a 100 mph the whole ride home. I whipped up in the driveway and ran in the house straight to the safe and majority of my money was gone.

"Fuck!" I yelled.

This money was the connect money. This hoe had me hot. I sat with my hands on my head and thought about where the fuck Jazmine could be. She wasn't stupid enough to stay in town. My phone started ringing, and I immediately grabbed it without looking at the phone

"Bitch, where are you at?" I yelled.

The voice on the phone spoke, and it wasn't Jazmine.

"Mr. Miles, um sorry this is Dr. Meridian, and we're calling to inform you that your father has passed away. We need you and your brother here at the hospital, please." My body went in shock, and I dropped the phone and cried.

"Hello sir, are you still there?" the doctor said.

"I'm on my way," I mumbled and hung up the phone. As soon as I put the phone down, it started ringing again, and it was Darnell

"I'm on the way now," I said into the phone.

Chapter 3

Darius

It had been a month since we buried our pops. The feeling was terrible losing someone you love and was extremely close to. It was something I wouldn't wish on my worst enemy. Jazmine's funky ass was still missing, but when my dad died, he left both Darnell and me a nice chunk of change along with all his belongings, so I was able to get the money replaced that Jazmine had taken from me. A nigga has been fucking off with Ebony. It was nothing too serious, a couple of dates here and there, and of course, she broke a nigga off. My trust ain't been right since Jazmine pulled that stunt on a nigga. I'd been knowing that bitch for years, and couldn't believe she'd pulled a stunt like that on me.

Jazmine

I felt bad for what I did to Darius, but he had it coming. I was going to leave town with the money, but I just rented me an apartment and had been laying low. I couldn't up and leave anyway because my brother needed me. He was locked up, and I'm all he got here besides his ex bitch. I looked at my phone and decided to check my voicemail that Darius had just left.

"Jazmine, bitch I swear when I find you, I'm gone fuck you up something awful. If you think you can steal from me and get away with it. You got another thing coming."

I deleted the voicemail and hung up the phone. I sat there thinking how the hell could I get out of this.

Ebony

I was tired as hell sitting here at my desk staring at the computer. I had stayed out with Darius all night. Darnell had blown my phone up most of the night, so I was thinking of something to tell him when he came in because I knew he was gone be on some other shit. Getting up, I walked in Darnell's office to leave some files on his desk. When I placed them there, I accidentally knocked a picture he had on his desk on the floor. Reaching down to pick the picture up, what I saw made my heart speed up. The picture was of both Darius and Darnell with Darnell's dad. *Why was Darius in this picture, were they related?*

"What are you doing?" Darnell said, startling me. I placed the picture back on the desk.

"I was bringing these files in here, and I had knocked this picture on the floor. Who's the guy in the picture?" I had to ask. Darnell walked over to his desk to sit down.

"That's my brother Darius," he said. *Shit.*

"Brother, I never knew you had a brother."

"I don't tell you everything, Ebony. Like you, where were you last night? I know you saw me calling!" Darnell snapped.

"Oh, so you want to go there. I was with Kim." The lie rolled off my tongue so freely.

"So you say," Darnell grunted. I wasn't about to deal with his mood. I turned to walk out of the office.

"Close the door behind you!" he called out.

As soon as I got back to my desk, I picked up the phone and called Kim.

"Hello," she answered.

"You would not believe the shit I'm about to tell you," I whispered.

"Oh my god, what now?"

"Darius and Darnell are brothers."

"What!" Kim shouted in the phone

"Yes, this is bullshit. I can't believe this shit."

"Well, you just have to stop seeing Darius. What are you going to do? Your name is bound to come up in a simple ego conversation between the two."

"I don't know, and Darnell is already acting shady because I been distant since fucking with Darius. I got to end this shit with Darius, and either come clean with him or pray that he doesn't say anything to Darnell."

"Well, you better think fast. Let me go. My boss is coming," Kim whispered.

Darius

I was on my way back from seeing my connect and decided I would call Ebony to see if she could get away for lunch later. I dialed Ebony's number.

"Hello. Boy, you know I'm not supposed to be on my personal phone," she answered.

"My bad, I was just trying to see if you could get away for lunch later?" I apologized.

"Yeah, I can do that. Where you want to meet?" she asked.

"We can meet at The Pharmacy."

"That's cool. See you then." Ebony smiled.

Darnell

Things were starting to get rocky between Ebony and I. This is where the time came for separating business and pleasure. I decided I would ask her to lunch. When I came out of the office, Ebony had just hung up the phone and was smiling hard.

"What got you so happy?" I asked.

"Oh, nothing just in a good mood."

"Good, well, I was gone see if you wanted to do lunch today?"

"Sure, we can do that. Let me move some things around," Ebony said.

"Cool."

***

Lunch with Ebony was great felt just like old times. It had been a while since we were able to hang out. I'm no fool. I knew somebody else was in the picture. I just didn't know who. I don't like to be played with, so I had to let her know, while I had the chance. I picked up the glass and took a sip, not taking my eyes off Ebony. Ebony smile.

"What?" she asked.

"I know there's somebody else. I don't know who, but I'm the not the type to share. So, you don't have to come clean, but you do need to know I'm not gone waste my time on you any longer no matter how I feel about you. So, you need to make a decision if you want to keep me around," I stated calmly.

Ebony's face was priceless. She was shocked.

"I don't see how things went from sugar to shit in a month's time. I know I been dealing with the death of my father, but that's even more reason for you to be here for me. So, the choice is yours, sweetheart."

I stood up from the table and placed the money for the check down. Ebony still was speechless as she watched me walk away.

Darius

I spent my day looking over distribution to the many dealers I had and making sure my money was right. I was trying to kill time, and I didn't want to drive all the way home then have to turn around and leave back out whenever Ebony called. I called Darnell to see if he was at home or still at the office. When he said he was at home, I decided to stop by until Ebony was ready. Darnell stayed in the middle of downtown in a high-rise condo. I enjoyed my peace and quiet when I go home. I don't see how this nigga stayed dead smack in the middle of the city. I guess it was so that he could be close to his job. This was some nice shit. I didn't know he was pulling in this much money from being a lawyer. Knocking on the door, I could hear his heavy footsteps nearing the door.

"What up youngin'?" Darnell said, letting me in.

"Man, nigga, you swear you're just so much older than me," I laughed.

Darnell shit was spotless. I figured he had OCD like me and pops. We walked into the living room and sat down.

"You want something to drink?" he asked.

"Yeah, fix me whatever you drink." Darnell poured two glasses of D'usse and handed me one.

"You must have had a long day drinking this shit." I laughed.

"Man, a nigga is slipping. I done let my feelings possibly get wrapped up in the wrong female." He sighed.

"Aw shit, Well, at least she ain't rob your ass and run off like Jazmine did, I swear the day I see her, we gone have a problem. But always go with your instinct about a bitch being the wrong one. Pops told me that shit," I mentioned.

Darnell ass was laughing at me because he knew that every time I mentioned Jazmine, I got pissed off.

"Shit was cool, but this past month, I know she's been fucking off. I told her ass that I knew and she had to make her mind up because I don't share shit," Darnell said.

We continued to talk for about an hour, and my phone beeped. It was Ebony telling me she was ready.

"Well, bro, I got to go. I got a dinner date with a fine little shorty. I'll hit you later," I said, hitting him up.

Jazmine

Sitting at the light on Fourth Avenue in a rental car, I was waiting for the light to change. Something caught my eye, and it happened to look like Darius walking into Jeff Ruby's Steakhouse. When I looked closer, it sure was Darius and Ebony. Ebony was my brother's ex-girlfriend.

"Well, well, well, I can't wait to tell my brother this shit."

Darius and Ebony were holding hands and looking like the perfect couple.

"So that's who got your time, Darius. Well, we will see how this goes," I said, pulling off.

Chapter 4

Ebony

I had decided to end it with Darius, but I didn't know how. I really like him, but I knew I loved Darnell. The whole time during dinner, I was waiting on the right moment to tell Darius I was involved with someone, but the time just never happened. I didn't want to ruin the moment. Maybe I can just text him afterwards to let him know I could no longer see him again.

Jazmine

It had been two whole days since I saw Darius and Ebony together. My brother had been in the hole, but I knew that once he got back to his cell phone, he would call me. I had been calling and playing on Darius' phone just to fuck with him. I was pissed, seeing him with Ebony. I knew my brother was gone go off. He'd did a lot of shit for her ass, and she just up and forget about him.

The ringing of my phone interrupted my train of thought. Looking at the screen, I was happy as hell my brother was finally calling.

"Hello," I answered.

"Sis, what up?" Jamal said.

"You tell me. Why was your ass in the hole?"

"Man, a punk ass C.O. wrote me up for some bullshit, but that ain't important. I got your text. What you got to tell me?" he asked, getting straight to it.

"So, guess who I saw out a couple of nights ago?"

"Who?"

"Your precious Ebony, but you wouldn't believe who she was all hugged up on."

"Man, come on sis who?" Jama impatiently asked.

"My ex Darius," I hissed.

"Word, so you think they involved?" Jamal asked.

"They were holding hands, and all hugged up like they were."

"This bitch got me fucked up. I'm in this bitch because of her ass, and she doesn't even answer the phone when a nigga calls, but she's out in these streets with the next nigga!" Jamal spat. I could tell by his voice that he was hurt and pissed off.

"That bitch is gone pay me for this shit. Just watch. I got the perfect plan. That nigga finna get hit twice. Did you put my half of the money in the bank and some on my books?" Jamal asked.

"Yeah, of course."

"Cool, cool, well I'm about to get off this phone. They're making rounds. I'll talk to you real soon," Jamal said.

"Ok. Love you, bruh," I told him.

"Love you too, sis," he said, and we hung up the phone.

I knew my brother was devastated. He had bent over backwards for Ebony because he loved her. He helped her out when she needed him most and look at how she repaid him.

Ebony

Today I was hanging with Darnell and was enjoying the day, which consisted of us doing nothing but laying around and watching movies. Darnell had left to go pick up something to eat. My phone rang, and I didn't recognize the number glancing at the screen. At first, I wasn't going to answer, but I did.

"Hello."

"A nigga got to call from another number for you to answer. Damn Eb, you're really doing a nigga dirty after all I done for you?" Jamal asked.

Fuck! I was dodging him, and this nigga put me on the spot.

"Jamal, what do you want?" I asked as if I wasn't the one who did him wrong. He laughed away his anger.

"What do I want? Oh, let me tell you what I want. You gone get me some money," Jamal demanded.

"Jamal, I don't have any money to put on your books," I lied.

"Books, bitch ain't nobody talking about no fucking books. You gone help me get some money out of Darius!" he yelled.

I swallowed hard. How in the hell did he know about Darius?

"Darius is not my boyfriend, not that it's any of your business."

"Look, I got some boys that are gone handle everything. You just get his ass to the address that I'm gone text you a week from today. Do as I say, or you will be dealt with. You owe me, Ebony, so don't fuck with me!" Jamal yelled and hung up in my face.

I sat there looking at the phone in shock thinking back to how in the hell I had gotten in this predicament.

I was a freshman in college, and I had just moved on campus glad to get away from home. I was a little fast paced, and I was involved with an older man, so the freedom was great. Everyone thought that I was staying on campus, but I was really staying with my boyfriend, well one of my boyfriends.

The last few months of my senior year of high school, my mom had got herself a new boyfriend. My mom always worked third shift, so I was left home alone the majority of the time. My mom's boyfriend always looked at me awkwardly, and one night he forced himself upon me, and after that, he constantly raped me.

That summer I had become pregnant by my older boyfriend. I decided to tell my mom what was going on with the rape to cover up for my boyfriend, so I blamed her boyfriend. My mom was furious and told me that I was lying and that her man wouldn't do no shit like that.

I had also been dating Jamal and told him what was going on. Jamal's mom told me I could stay with them until I went off to college in August. My older boyfriend found out about Jamal and kicked me out after making me get an abortion.

One day, Jamal took me to my house to get some of my things. While we were in the house, my mom's boyfriend had come home trying to fight both Jamal and me. In a panic, I grabbed my mom's gun and shot him.

Before the police got there, Jamal told me to tell the police that her boyfriend was trying to rape me and that he had shot him. Jamal was charged because he was on probation, and of course, he wasn't supposed to have a gun in his possession. Jamal took his charge because he loved me. I went off to college and Jamal had become a distant memory after a year because I was focused on my real plan.

Breaking out of my trance, I heard Darnell come into the house with our food.

"You ready to eat, baby?" Darnell asked me. I shook off my thoughts and walked into the kitchen to eat.

"Yeah baby, I'm starving." I smiled. We sat down at the counter and ate while having light conversation.

Darius

I was chilling at the crib with my nigga Cam. Cam was a businessman, and I was considering flipping properties like Cam did. He had a chain of businesses all around Nashville and Atlanta. I needed places to invest and hide my money, so Cam was the man for the job.

"Cam, I'm really serious about this. I need to get this money cleaned, but I need a business that I can also be hands-on in. Eventually, this drug shit is gone be pushed down to where I won't be getting my hands dirty. So, I want businesses that are pulling in money," I told Cam.

Cam nodded.

"I got you whatever you need from clubs and restaurants to retail. Shit, I can even get your name backgrounded into something that's already established. You just need to put so much money into a company, which will make you part owner. Have you ever thought about buying half of your brother's firm?" Cam asked.

"Hell, I didn't think of that. Darnell might be cool with that. I'm gone ask him," I said.

"That will for sure be a good investment," Cam suggested.

"So how life treating you? How are Charisma and the kids?" I asked.

"Life's great, I can't complain. They're doing good. Speaking of which, Charisma said she had seen Jazmine a couple of days ago at the nail shop. What's going on with y'all?" Cam asked.

I filled him in on what Jazmine had done and how I'd been looking for her.

"Damn dog, I wish we had known. You know Charisma's crazy ass would've beat the brakes off her had she known. I'm gone tell Charisma this shit just in case she runs into her again," Cam said.

"That bitch needs more than an ass whooping," I fumed, causing us both to start laughing.

Ebony

A Week Later

I was sitting at my desk in a daze when my cell phone rang. I looked at the phone and knew it was Jamal. I sighed and answered the phone.

"Yes, Jamal."

"Tonight at 8:45. The address was just sent to your phone," he said and hung up.

I rolled my eyes, looked at the phone, and saw the address. Now I was thinking how in the hell do they know if Darius will have enough money on him for them to rob him. Knowing Jamal, I bet his little goons had been watching Darius like a hawk and knew his every move. I sent Darius a text asking could he pick me up when he was heading home tonight, and that I wanted to spend the night with him, and of course, he said he would.

Darius

I was finishing my last rounds before I headed home. Ebony wanted to hang out, so I had to stop and get her. I called Ebony to let her know that I would be heading her way in about fifteen minutes because I was running behind. When I looked at the time, it was 8:40. I was sitting at the stop sign looking at some shit on my phone when my driver side window shattered.

"Nigga, come on up off that loot!" one of the mask guys yelled while another hopped in the passenger side.

"Nigga, ain't no cash in here," I said calmly. The dude hopped in the backseat.

"Pull off!" he demanded. I pulled off and laughed

"Y'all niggas must don't know who the hell I am," I said.

"Nigga, we don't give a fuck who you are, but you're about to come up off that loot before your brains paint the inside of this nice ass truck," the masked guy said.

"Pull over right here!" the guy yelled. I did as I was told and pulled over.

"Now, give us the money before shit gets serious," he demanded.

I couldn't get out of this situation with it being two against one and a gun on me. I pulled the small bag from under my seat and handed it to the guy.

"Good, we ain't got to kill your ass. Nice doing business with you partner," the guy said and hit my ass with the butt of the gun before exiting the truck. The guys ran off in the other direction.

I put the truck in drive and drove to Ebony's house.

"Fuck!" I yelled.

I was beyond pissed this the second damn time, I done got hit. I pulled up and hopped out my truck and knocked on Ebony's door. Ebony opened the door.

"Oh my god, Darius what happened?" she cried.

"Man, some niggas just robbed my ass," I huffed. I sat down on the couch as Ebony ran off. I called my homie Clint.

Ebony

When I saw Darius, I thanked God that they hit him before he got here. I ran to the bathroom to get him some things to clean his face. When I came back to the living room, Darius was on the phone.

"Hell yeah man, somebody's been watching me. Them niggas hit me soon as I left both spots. I bet Jazmine's bitch ass had something to do with this shit," he said deep into his conversation.

My ears perked up at the mention of Jazmine's name. I wonder if he's talking about Jamal's sister Jazmine. I walked over and started cleaning Darius' face. He finished his call with Clint before giving me his attention.

"I don't mean to pry but who is Jazmine?" I asked.

"My ex-girlfriend, her conniving ass robbed me before she left, and I ain't seen her ass since. Now, all of a sudden this shit happens again. I bet this got her name all on it!" Darius snapped.

"Oh," was all I said. *This damn city is too fucking small.*

Chapter 5

Darius

I was stressed out after the robbery because I hated not knowing who in the hell was responsible for this shit. I'm a nigga that always moves carefully and to be caught slipping was fucking with me. I told Cam to make sure that Charisma keeps an eye out for Jazmine's funky ass. Everything I did had to be changed up— days I moved shipments, did pick-ups, and I even moved all the spots. I even hired someone to follow me 24/7 I wasn't taking any more losses. I wasn't beefing with nobody in Nashville. My name rang bells. I was respected and made sure everybody ate, so if it wasn't Jazmine, I didn't know who was behind this shit.

Ebony

My head was hurting because I was still trying to piece together everything. I was glad that I wasn't in the car with Darius. The thing that bothered me most was I didn't know Jazmine was dealing with Darius or better yet had already robbed him. This had Jamal's name all over it.

I was in the breakroom at work brewing a pot of coffee, trying to remain normal after all that had gone down. Darnell was aware of the situation because he had loaned Darius some money. My cell phone started to ring, and it was Jamal.

"What Jamal? I'm at work," I seethed.

"I need another favor," Jamal said.

"Have you lost your damn mind? I'm not doing shit else for you. I don't care what you try to hang over my head. I'm done with your ass. Setting up Darius was enough. I'm sure you got enough cash out of it, so leave me the fuck alone, and don't call this phone no fucking more!" I snapped and hung up the phone.

Darnell

It was early, and I had to be at court in an hour for my morning docket. I was about to enter the breakroom when I heard Ebony on the phone. Listening to her conversation had me heated.

Who the fuck is Jamal? I thought. Was this the nigga that had her attention? She set up my brother? How? So many questions were unanswered.

Entering the breakroom, I cleared my throat.

"Ebony, I need to see you in my office right now," I said walking out and headed back to my office.

I could feel her following closely behind me. We entered my office, and I closed the door. I instantly started to pace the floor thinking about what all I heard.

"What's the problem?" Ebony asked.

"Who is Jamal and don't fucking lie to me?" I said through clenched teeth. Ebony swallowed hard

"I don't know what you're talking about," Ebony lied. Making sure she felt me, I stepped to her face and looked her dead in the eyes.

"Don't insult me. I just heard your entire phone conversation and seeing that I had to come out of my pocket to help my brother, your motherfucking ass better start singing."

"Look, Darnell. It's not what you think, Jamal is my ex, and he's in jail. He was blackmailing me if I didn't set Darius up. That's all, and I asked him to leave me alone," Ebony cried.

Her tears didn't move me, and I felt she was lying.

"What you are saying doesn't even sound right. How does this nigga even know my brother?" I asked.

"I don't know, maybe because he is Jazmine's brother," Ebony said.

"Most importantly, how and why would he come to you to set my brother up? You don't even know my brother like that. What's this Jamal's guy last name?" I asked.

"Jones," Ebony said.

"I think I need to pay Mr. Jones a visit because you are clearly not telling me everything," I said, sitting on the desk. Ebony walked over and stood between my legs and placed her arms around my neck.

"I have nothing to hide from you," she said.

Darius

Cam had given me some paperwork, and I wanted my brother to look over them, so I stopped by his job. Entering his office, no one was sitting at the front desk. I was expecting a warm greeting from Ebony, so I headed straight to my brother's office. When I opened the door, Ebony was standing in between my brother's legs and her arms around his neck.

"Well damn, excuse me!" I called out. Ebony almost shitted herself. Darnell stood up and adjusted himself.

"You ever heard of knocking, damn nigga?" he said. Ebony was making her way out of the office, and I blocked her way.

"You're in such a hurry that you can't speak?" I asked with lifted brows.

"Hi Darius, excuse me. I got to get back to work," she nervously responded exiting the office — *shiesty bitch.*

"Damn, bro, please tell me you ain't hitting that?" I asked Darnell. Inquiring minds wanted to know.

"Ebony is my girlfriend, nigga. I just can't be broadcasting that shit around the office," Darnell said.

"Ain't this some shit."

"What are you going on about?" Darnell asked.

"Ebony is the chick I've been fucking off with. Nigga, you said y'all wasn't involved." Darnell looked at me like I was crazy.

"What?" he said.

"This shit wild. Shit, when you said you weren't fucking with ole gal, I ran into her one night, and shit, we've been talking ever since. She said she was single. I've been smashing that, bruh." I laughed.

Darnell sat there with a disturbed look in his face.

"This bitch just full of secrets!" he spat.

"Look bruh, I ain't mean no harm. I didn't know. I wouldn't do no sour shit like that."

"It's all good. I'm gone handle that. What is it that you needed?" Darnell sighed.

"Oh, just look into this paperwork for me before I put my signature on it," I informed him, handing him the papers.

"Aite, I gotcha. I'll get to it before the day is over, and I give you a call."

"Thanks, bruh," I said, dapping him up. When I left out of there, I walked up to Ebony sitting at her desk

"You a scandalous ass bitch, and Darnell knows everything. My brother deserves better!" I snapped and walked off.

Darnell

Staring off into space, I sat at my desk with my hand underneath my chin, thinking about what the hell just happened. All this shit I found out in a day's time was entirely too much. I was going to get to the bottom of this other shit first before I dealt with Ebony ass. I typed Jamal Jones in the database to see where he was being held. It was time I paid this nigga a little visit. I grabbed my jacket and headed out of the office. When I walked by Ebony, I just shook my head.

***

Arriving at CCA, I walked in and went straight to see the warden. He was cool, and I had a standing relationship with him.

"Hello, Warden," I reached out shaking the warden's hand.

"Mr. Taylor, it's nice to see. Sorry about your father," the warden said giving his condolences.

"Thank you."

"So, what can I help you with today?"

"I need to speak with a Jamal Jones. I might be picking up his case, depending on how this interview goes," I told the warden a small fib.

"Oh, I got you. Let me call down and get him up here for you."

"Appreciate that."

The warden got on the phone and made the call.

"He will be up shortly."

A few minutes later Jamal was entering the warden's office. The C.O. led him in, and the warden stood.

"I'll leave y'all to it," he said, walking out the office.

I stood and faced Jamal.

"Who are you supposed to be?" Jamal asked.

"Depending on how you respond to my questions, I might be the one to get you out of here."

"I need to know your dealings with Ebony." I just came right on out. Jamal chuckled.

"Man, you come here to check me about a bitch?" Jamal said.

"That bitch is my bitch. What's your history with her, and why are you trying to blackmail her?"

"Your bitch, you must not know the real Ebony. She is everybody bitch. Damn, I thought that was Darius bitch." Jamal laughed.

"Wrong again, and if you want to be a free man, I suggest you start fucking talking."

Jamal took a seat.

"Ebony used to be my gal. I thought she was the one. I would've done anything for her, as you can see that's why I'm here. Ebony was finna go off to college until her mom got a new boyfriend. He had started messing with her, she got pregnant, and her mom put her out. My mom took her in until she went off to college. So, one day we went to her house to get her things, and dude popped up trying to fight on her and shit, so I jumped in, and we started fighting. Ebony got her mom's gun and shot dude. We changed the story, and when the cops came, I told them I did it. With me being on papers, they weren't trying to hear shit. I thought Ebony was gone be here for a nigga, but when she went off to college, she forgot about a nigga." Jamal sighed, coming clean.

I took in all that he said.

"Pregnant, what happened to the baby, and why did you make her set up this Darius guy?"

"She had an abortion, and man that nigga got what he deserved. He fucked over my sister and took my girl, so it was the perfect thing to do." Jamal shrugged.

"If I remember correctly your sister robbed him, and technically, I took your girl. After I walk out of here, stay the fuck away from Ebony and leave her alone. I'll be in contact about your case," I said, leaving it at that.

Hell, yeah I'm gone get that nigga out, he just doesn't know what I got in store for his ass though.

***

When I got back to the office, Ebony was trying to look busy I knew she was nervous, not knowing what I had up my sleeve.

"Ms. Rose, I need to see you in my office."

"Yes sir," Ebony said, getting up immediately. She closed the door behind her and stood in front of my desk while I took a seat.

"I just left from seeing your friend Jamal. I will be working on his release, so I need you to get his case for me so that I can start on that asap," I insisted.

Ebony's mouth dropped.

"What do you mean you are getting him out?" Ebony asked in shock.

"Why should he stay in jail if you pulled the trigger?" I said, trying to shake Ebony up.

"When he is released, you don't have to worry about him bothering you. Oh, stay the hell away from my brother also. I would hate to have you arrested for the murder of your mom's boyfriend."

Ebony eyes bulged.

"Are you serious, Darnell? That man raped me, so he got what he deserved," Ebony quizzed.

"Yeah, I heard, but it's your word against a dead man's. You know I can make things happen."

Ebony rubbed her temples, and I knew now that ass was stressed and scared.

"Darnell, for what's it worth, I'm sorry for all this. I really do love you, and I never meant to hurt you," Ebony issued a half-ass apology.

The thing was I loved her too. I was just furious as hell, so I wasn't sure exactly what I was thinking. Hell, I needed time.

"Apology accepted, now I need to finish up. Close the door when you leave." Ebony turned to walk out of the office

"I love you too," I mumbled in a whisper that only I could hear.

Chapter 6

Jazmine

I'm not sure what exactly happened, but when my brother called and told me he was being released, I ain't ask no questions and I was there to see him walk out them gates. He was finally a free man

I leaned against the car, and when he saw my face, his smile widened.

"What up, baby sis!" he yelled.

"Welcome home, bruh." Hugging him, I had so many emotions running through me.

"I brought you some clothes. I'm sure you want to head to the mall in something fresh. I also took you some money out so that you can pick you up some things at the mall," I told him. He knew I had his back.

"Thanks for looking out sis. Thanks for sitting on this money too," Jamal said.

"No problem. You know I got you," Jazmine said.

Cam

Clint and I were at the barbershop in my office having a conversation about some gal Clint's ass was talking to. This nigga was happy as hell that he'd finally hooked him a bad one. Clint handed me his phone showing me a picture of her on Facebook. I grabbed the phone and looked at the picture. She was a decent little chick, not my type. It was a habit for me to scroll through Clint's Facebook feed because my ass didn't have a page.

"Yo, Clint, look at this shit," I said showing the picture of Clint's lil chick posing with Jamal and Jazmine at the mall. The caption read *Welcome Home Mal*.

"Who is this nigga Mal?" I asked.

"That's Jamal, Jazmine's brother." My antennas went off while I was rubbing my beard.

"It's some shit in the game, peep this. The other day it was some nigga's in here chopping it up, and I heard that nigga's name and Darius' name in the same sentence talking about dude was coming home to a nice chunk of change, and you just said that Jazmine is his sister? You know Darius said he thinks Jazmine had something to do with that second robbery. I'm gone holla at dude's homeboy and see if he talks. Don't say shit to Darius until I find out for sure what's going on," I told Clint.

Clint nodded his head.

In due time, the average man will eventually tell on himself in some type of way, especially when they feel they have a point to prove.

Jamal made his entrance into the barbershop feeling cocky as hell.

"They let a nigga out!" he called out, throwing his hands up.

Clint and I were chopping it up when I looked over at the camera, after being notified the door opened. If I wasn't on the floor, I made sure I saw everyone who stepped foot in my shit from my office.

"Well, look what we have here!" I nodded pointing to the monitor. Leaning forward, I turned the sound.

"They let a nigga out!" he heard Jamal say. *This nigga is bound to talk, typical jerk nigga shit.*

"Nigga, how you get out?" the barber asked Jamal.

"I got people that got clout. My lawyer Mr. Taylor got me out with all charges dropped," Jamal said, rubbing his hands together.

Both Clint and I looked at each other like *what the fuck* when we heard Darius' brother name.

"What happened to ole gal that you were with before you got knocked?"

"Shit, I thought she was the one. She helped me with a lick while I was in there, but shit, she with the lawyer that got me out." He laughed.

"I'm not even finna ask how that happen. Nigga your shit sounds like a damn Tyler Perry movie," the barber joked.

"I'm just speaking the truth," Jamal said.

I couldn't even believe the shit that I was hearing.

"So, this nigga is saying that Darnell messes with Ebony, and Ebony set Darius up, and Darnell got Jamal out of jail. This shit is making my head hurt, bruh."

"Shit, that's what it sounds like, but you can't put shit past folks in Nashville. You know they messy as hell here," Clint said.

"I just don't think Darnell would do his brother like that. It's got to be something else to this shit. As soon that nigga leaves the shop, call Darius and get him down here," I told Clint.

Darius

Clint called me and told me I needed to come down to the shop because it was important, so I was in route. Sitting at the red light, nodding my head to that new Don Trip, I could've sworn I saw Jazmine ride by. I shook the thought out of my head thinking it couldn't be her, but ever since I was robbed, a nigga stayed on my Ps and Qs. I looked up in my rearview mirror to make sure my security was behind me. I whipped in the parking lot, stepped out, and dapped a few niggas up that was standing outside the shop.

"What's up?" I spoke as I made my way through the shop to the back. Cam and Clint were sitting there with stress all over both their faces.

"What's up, everything good?" I asked, sitting down.

"That's what we are trying to figure out," Cam said.

"Whatever happened to that girl Ebony you were messing with?"

"I cut her off. I found out that she was my brother's girl. Why?"

"Word on the street is Jazmine brother Jamal got out, but Jamal was the one behind your robbery. He had Ebony set you up. The worst part is Darnell was the one to get this nigga charges dropped and released," Cam said.

I looked at both Clint and Cam.

"Where did y'all niggas hear this shit at?" I was pissed off.

"Cam heard some niggas bragging and then that nigga Jamal came in here today saying the same shit. I got that nigga on camera." Clint said.

What the hell? I was boiling. This couldn't be true. It had to be a lie.

"Nah, my brother ain't on no shit like that," I said in disbelief.

"I know the shit sounds crazy, but this shit is running together, bruh."

"I'm going to get to the bottom of this!" I spat, storming out of the office.

The more I thought about it the shit was making sense. I texted my brother asking him where he was at. Darnell texted back saying he was at home. Hopping straight on the interstate, I headed straight to

Darnell's. I ain't give a fuck about no neighbors or none of that shit as I beat on his door.

"Yo, man what the hell is your problem, beating on my door like you crazy?" Darnell spat when he yanked the door opened. I rushed in and walked past Darnell, and I saw Ebony standing in the kitchen. I chuckled and turned to my brother

"So, you still messing with this bum ass bitch after all she did?" I fumed.

"Bitch, who you are calling a bitch?" Ebony spat. This hoe was gone feel me.

"Bitch, I ought to choke the shit out of you right here."

"Hold up, you not finna keep disrespecting her in my face, what's the problem?" Darnell asked.

"How can you stay with somebody that crossed your own blood? You knew this bitch set me up, then you turn around and help the nigga behind the shit get out of jail. I just know my own brother ain't on no grimy shit."

"It's not what you think. I swear it's not. Ebony only did that because the dude was threatening her. Yeah, I got him out, but I have my reasons. You just got to trust me on this," Darnell said.

"Really, trust you? After you kept this shit from me?"

My brother sighed and rubbed his head looking back over his shoulder at Ebony.

"Look, I promise you just give me some time. This is gone work out in your favor, baby bruh. Just let me handle this," Darnell pleaded.

I looked at his brother and with no response turned and walked out.

Ebony

This nigga was too disrespectful, thank God Darnell was here, but now I'm trying to figure out what Darnell meant by what he said to his brother.

"Darnell, I don't know what you got up your sleeve, but I won't be a part of it. This shit is just one big ass mess," I told him.

Darnell faced me.

"Oh, you're already in this. The moment you fucked my brother and set him up, you were put in this big ass mess."

"Look, Darnell. I love you and all, but I'm not gone allow you to throw that in my face every time you see fit. I will leave before I allow you to keep talking to me any kind of way."

"If that's how you feel, I'm not stopping you, but you owe me remember, or you want to go to jail?"

Darius

My brother had me fucked up. I couldn't make sense of the situation, but I was gone let my brother do whatever he needed to do. For some reason, I just couldn't understand why my brother was still dealing with Ebony though. She was dirty and has been from the jump.

I was in desperate need of a drink, so I stopped at La Parilla. Taking a seat at the bar, I didn't even need a menu. The bartender made her way over to me,

"Let me get a Hennessey on the rocks, please."

"I know I'm good for a round?" I heard a girl say. I turned around, and it was Cam's wife Charisma.

"Hey, girl, yeah you're fam, so you can get anything you want," I told her. Charisma sat down beside me.

"Nigga you looked stressed, what's up?" she asked.

"Man, a nigga is. There is too much shit going on."

"Cam told me about the Jazmine situation, do know that when I see her, I'm gone handle that for you," Charisma said.

"I appreciate that I can't seem to run into that bitch nowhere, but her time coming."

Chapter 7

Darnell

My first task was getting Ebony on board with what I was planning. When I found out what Jamal did, I put my plan into motion the moment that I told Jamal I would get him out. I knew my brother was skeptical, and I hated that Darius didn't believe me when I told him I had everything taken care of.

Ebony was sitting on the couch pouting. I made my way over to her taking a seat beside her. Reaching down, I picked up her hand and placed it in mine. Ebony was a sight, and her beauty was unmatched. I just starred at her taking it all in, I loved her, but deep down inside I couldn't erase the image of her sleeping with my brother.

"Ebony, can we talk?" I asked. She still had an attitude.

"That depends on what about," she sassed.

"Look, I deserve the attitude, but baby be real. How do you expect me to forget all that you did?" I asked.

Ebony looked down, and I placed my finger underneath her chin and lifted her head.

"Just tell me what made you sleep with my brother, I mean were you trying to pursue something serious?"

"I didn't know he was your brother, not that it makes it any better, but I honestly don't know. He started off flirting, and he approached me. When he asked if I was seeing someone, I didn't want to tell him about you exposing our secret because at the time I wasn't aware that he was your brother or the type of relationship y'all had. I know it was wrong. It was just something to do," Ebony paused.

"I know this makes me look bad and like a liar, but Darnell, I love you, always have, and still do. I just need another chance to show you that I'm sorry. Jamal put me in a bind. I can't go to jail, so I did what he asked. I was really supposed to be in the car with Darius and take him somewhere, but they were watching him that whole entire week and just caught him slipping," Ebony admitted.

"I need you to help me get Jamal back. I want to rob that nigga and let Darius handle the rest. You gone have to get close to him again."

"Get close to him how?"

"I don't know. Make him start trusting you again. Don't sleep with him, but do whatever else you got to do. I'll handle the rest."

Ebony had this look in her eyes as if she was turned on. She leaned in for a kiss, and my lips met hers. I knew this shit was wrong, but I couldn't resist. Ebony got up placing herself in my lap facing me, and our tongues continued to dance like it was the last one. I lifted Ebony and carried her to the bedroom. Laying her on the bed, her bedroom eyes didn't leave mine as I removed my shirt. Tossing it, I climbed in the bed and started kissing the inside of her thighs.

That's when it hit me again that my brother had been inside of her and there was no way I was putting my mouth back on her. Ebony grabbed the back of my head, trying to lead me to water, but I couldn't do it. Lifting myself, I leaned over and grabbed a condom from the nightstand sliding it on. I propped Ebony up in the exact position I wanted her in and slid inside.

Ebony moans were growing louder, and here I was trying to think of something else to keep me hard. How my mood changed was crazy as hell. Ebony's ass was bouncing back on my dick and visions of her and Darius fucking was blocking my nut. With each thought, I grew angry, and Ebony was matching it.

"Fuck!" I spat, pulling out. My shit went on limp.

Ebony looked behind at me as if she was pissed. I wasn't in no mood to argue, and if she knew what was good, she bet not say shit. Ebony collapsed on the side of me.

"I need you to start working on Jamal like yesterday. If you can get close to Jazmine to that would be helpful," I blurted out.

"What you got planned?"

"Now why would I tell you that?" I asked, laughing.

"I just thought it would be nice to know."

"Well don't worry, I'll tell you when the time is right."

Darius

"Bruh, come the fuck on and throw the ball!" I yelled at the TV. I was playing *Madden* to take my mind off shit.

"Boss, there's a female visitor here wanting to see you," my security Red barged in interrupting.

"Who is it?" I asked not even taking my eyes off the game.

"She said her name was Jazmine, sir," Red replied.

My head whipped around fast as hell at the mention of her name. I placed the controller down and hopped off the couch.

"This bitch got her nerve," I said, walking to the door. Opening the door, sho nuff it was Jazmine.

"You got a lot of nerve showing up on my doorstep!" I spat.

Jazmine looked down at her feet and rubbed her hands down the side of her jeans as if she was nervous.

"Darius, I know you are very angry at me and probably don't want to hear nothing I have to say, but can we please talk?" she spoke.

Talking was the last thing on my mind, but I did want to hear her out.

"Red, search her," I demanded. Red did as he was told and checked Jazmine thoroughly.

She had a very large purse, and Red looked inside with widened eyes he handed me her purse. Looking inside, I was shocked to see all this money.

"What the hell is this?" I asked Jazmine.

"If you would please just allow me a few minutes to talk to you, I will tell you all that," Jazmine said. I moved out of the way to allow Jazmine to come completely in the house.

"Red stay close by the door." Red nodded his big head in agreement and stood outside the door.

"Talk!" I yelled.

"Darius, I am sorry first and foremost. I don't know why I did what I did, but it was stupid as hell on my part. I did not have anything to do with that second robbery. That was my brother doing. I did lie to him a while back telling him you were mistreating me and shit. I didn't think all this was gone come from that," Jazmine said.

She reached for the bag I was holding and pulled out the money.

"This is what I took and a little bit more to cover what I spent," Jazmine said. Looking at the money, I grabbed it out of Jazmine's hand. Just by eyeballing it, I could tell that it was all there.

"Where did you get this, Jazmine?" I had to ask.

"I really didn't spend much, and what I did spend, I kind of took it from my brother." Jazmine shrugged.

To hear her say that made me soften a little bit. Jazmine had returned all my money plus a little bit more. She stole from her own brother. *But why?*

"Why are you doing this, Jazmine?" Jazmine stepped a little closer to me.

"I had to make things right, and I couldn't bring a child into this world under these circumstances," she said.

"What!"

"I'm pregnant, Darius," Jazmine mumbled. On first instinct, I looked down at Jazmine's stomach.

"I'm only three months," she answered, I guess figuring out what I was thinking. I had so many emotions inside of me that I didn't know how to react.

"This just complicates things even more now. You do know your brother still took from me and could've had me killed, and now you're pregnant. This will not stop me from getting back what's mine or taking certain measures against your brother. Then when shit pops off, you're caught in the mix because you are carrying my child," I reassured her.

"Darius, I just stole from my own brother to pay you your money. My concern is this child in my stomach. Jamal knew what he was dealing with when he decided to do it. I'm here with you, and I have nothing to do with you and my brother."

"So, you gone tell me where that nigga at?" I asked.

Jazmine shook her head.

"Nope, Jamal will show his face in due time," Jazmine said.

Ebony

Awakening the next morning, my head was killing me. Stress was a motherfucker. I thought long and hard about what I was going to do to Jamal. Looking over, Darnell was sleeping peacefully. With each breath he took I watched the rise and fall of his chest. Biting my bottom lip, I thought hard about last night's conversation. What I had to do was hard, but I owed him. Easing out of bed, I slipped my feet in my slippers and headed to the bathroom so that I could take a shower and get ready for the day.

My life was built on a lie from the beginning. This all started as a revenge/ get back scheme but had evolved in to so much more. When I got out of the shower, I threw on a pair of leggings and a hoodie. Before walking out the door, I looked back at Darnell still sleeping peacefully and walked out of the house.

Once in the car, I pulled off and dialed a number. The person answered on the first ring.

"Yeah!" the person said.

"Are you at home? We need to talk?" I asked.

"Yeah."

"I'm on the way," I said and hung up the phone.

Chapter 8

Ebony

Arriving at my destination, I grabbed my purse and exited the car. I knocked on the door twice. I could hear the footsteps growing closer to the door

"Who is it?" the voice said.

"Me," I replied. The door opened, and I walked in.

"Damn, I can't get no hug?" the voice asked. I turned around and hugged him.

"Long time no see," he said.

"It has been a minute, hasn't it?"

"Longer than a minute, what brings you by?"

"Darnell is planning something, I don't know exactly what it is, but his whole reason to get you out was to get you back for what you did to his brother, I said.

There was an awkward silence.

"Jamal, did you hear what I just said?"

"Yeah, let that nigga go ahead with his plans, at least let him think you're doing whatever it is he asked you to do," Jamal said, shaking his head as he thought. He continued to look at me strangely.

"Don't tell me you done actually fell for this nigga, son? You were supposed to get what was yours for that nigga cutting you out the will before he died," Jamal reminded me.

The truth was I was Daryll's little young thing he had on the side. I knew all about Darius and Darnell before they knew about each other. When Daryll found out he had prostate cancer, I was the one there for him in the early stages before he told his sons what was going on. I was never pregnant by my mom's boyfriend. I was pregnant by Daryll.

Daryll made me get the abortion and shortly after he cut me out of his will when he discovered I was involved with Jamal. My mom's boyfriend was raping me and me shooting him, that much of the story was true.

I decided to get in where I fit in with Darnell, and everything seemed to be falling into place until Jamal wanted to become greedy.

"Ebony!" Jamal called out, breaking me out of my trance

"I heard you, Jamal. Things just starting to be messed up. It wasn't supposed to go this far. I just wanted the money Daryll fucked me out of. He did me dirty when I was there for him. I killed my baby for that nigga," I cried.

"Look, don't worry about me. You just try to stay focus and do what you need to do." Jamal said.

Jamal never liked the fact that I was messing around on him with Daryll. I stood up, and before leaving, I turned to Jamal

"Be careful!" I said, wrapping my arms around his neck hugging him.

Jamal stood still for a second guess he was shocked, I could feel his hesitation, but he put his arms around me and hugged me back.

Jazmine

Darius and I were sitting at the kitchen table having breakfast when I got a text from my brother saying that we needed to talk. I was hoping that it wasn't about the money I stole. I looked up from my plate and looked at Darius. I was happy. I made the right decision and glad to be back home.

"I'm going to see my brother today. He claims we need to talk," I told Darius. Darius nodded.

"Don't tell that nigga we back together," Darius said chewing his food.

"I'm not. I hope he ain't finna ask me about that money."

"If he does, tell that nigga you don't know shit. You know how to play it," Darius said.

He scooted back from the table finished with his breakfast, before walking over to me. I had barely touched my food.

"You need to eat, Jazmine. You are eating for two now. You barely touch your food," Darius voiced.

"I barely eat in the mornings because I'm just gone throw it right back up." I sighed, already over this pregnancy. Darius took the plates in the kitchen. I gathered my things and called out to Darius.

"I'll call you as soon as I leave." He just nodded his head.

I was praying the entire ride over that Jamal didn't ask me about the money. My hands were getting sweaty holding the steering wheel, so I turned the air on to cool my body temperature down. Getting off the exit, the closer I got, my stomach started turning. Pulling into the yard, it was no turning back. When I knocked on the door, I could hear my heart beat loudly.

"What up, little sis?" Jamal smiled, opening the door.

"Hey," I said trying not to seem nervous. I sat down across from him and sat my purse in my lap.

"Where your ass been at? You ain't stay here last night, and you didn't call," Jamal asked.

"I stayed at my home girl's house and didn't feel like driving last night. Damn, you ain't my daddy." I laughed.

"Whatever. Anyway, guess who just left from over here?"

"Who?"

"Ebony. Check this out. She said that nigga Darnell got me out on purpose and that he was planning some shit for his brother Darius," Jamal laughed.

I swallowed hard, and my mouth flew open.

"I'm confused, why would she tell you that? Ain't she with him?"

Jamal lit his cigarette.

"It's some shit you don't know about Ebony. She's been playing both them brothers from the jump. She used to date they old man. When he got sick, she was there for that nigga, and then he did her dirty. He cut her out of the will and made her abort his baby. In my opinion, he did what any other nigga would do when they find out they gal ain't shit." Jamal shrugged.

"Damn," I whispered, taking in all this shit. I couldn't wait to get back and tell Darius.

"What are you gone do?" I asked Jamal.

"I ain't gone do shit. Them niggas can bring whatever heat they need. I told Ebony to go ahead and do whatever it is he asks her," Jamal said getting loud like he was feeling himself.

"Well, be careful, Jamal," I said.

Darnell

I was at my office getting ready for a court hearing. My office phone rang.

"Mr. Taylor speaking," I answered.

"I heard you were looking for me. There's no need for a setup. Anytime you ready for a nigga, you can always call, and we can meet up," Jamal said laughing and hung up.

Looking at the receiver in my hand, I scrunched my face. I knew it was Jamal, but how in the hell Jamal know what's going on. Where the fuck was Ebony at? She had been gone all morning. I picked up the phone and dialed Ebony's number.

"Hey, babe," Ebony answered. I kept my cool,

"Where you at? I haven't heard from you since you left this morning. You got a nigga worried."

"Oh, I've been working on what you told me to work on," Ebony said, not knowing about the phone call I had just got.

I shook my head.

"Aw ok, well I'll be at the office for a little bit preparing for this case."

"Do I need to come in?" Ebony asked.

"No, keep doing whatever it is you've been doing. I'll talk to you later," I said quickly hanging up the phone.

Something wasn't right with Ebony. Why would she tell Jamal that shit and why is she trying to play a nigga? What is it that Ebony is keeping from me?

Jazmine

Darius and I met up for lunch at Party Fowl. He was standing out front waiting for me to park my car. When I walked up on Darius, he was busy on his phone looking like a nice piece of candy. He was dressed in denim jeans and a solid white YSL collar shirt. He smiled as I walked closer to him.

"What's up, baby?" he greeted me. I leaned in and kissed him.

"Nothing much, I'm actually hungry since I didn't eat much this morning." We walked inside of Party Fowl's and stood in line. Once Darius got off the phone, I turned to him.

"So, you want to wait to after you eat to hear the news or now because after I tell you, you're probably not gone be able to sit still," I indicated.

Darius sighed.

"Is it that crucial?" Darius asked.

I nodded my head.

"You might as well go ahead and tell me since you brought it up," Darius said. We moved up a little in line, and I leaned in so Darius could hear what I was finna say

Ebony is on some sneaky shit."

"Ebony?" Darius asked. My lips curled a bit, and I nodded my head yes.

"Yep Ebony. She told my brother that Darnell was setting him up from the jump, from getting him out up until now. Darnell's got something planned and asked Ebony to get close to Jamal for him," I confessed.

"That nigga was telling the truth," Darius said.

"What the fuck Ebony got going on though, first me then my brother. From what I know, my brother had been nothing but good to her. I know this nigga loves her ass," Darius hissed.

The lined moved up, and we ordered some hot chicken. Darius paid for our food while I found somewhere for us to sit. When Darius came to the table, we both started in on our food.

"You ready to hear the rest?" Darius nodded and took a sip of his drink.

"Ebony is doing this to get back at your dad," I slowly said. I was scared to tell him that part.

"What the fuck my pops got to do with any of this shit?" Darius seethed.

I swatted at Darius' hand to get him to calm down

"Sssh, supposedly Ebony was involved with your dad rather seriously sometime before he died. She claimed that when your father was first diagnosed with cancer before he even told y'all, she was by his side, and she had gotten pregnant, but he made her get an abortion because he had found out about Jamal. He then cut her off completely and changed the will and everything. So, she set out to get her revenge through you and your brother," I expressed.

Darius damn near choked on his chicken he was so thrown by what I just said.

"Darius," I called out.

No answer.

"Darius," I said again. Darius blinked

"Yeah?" he said.

"You ok?"

"I'm gone be just fine. I got to get to my brother and talk to him."

Chapter 9

Darnell

My brother called me asking me to meet up, so I was sitting outside of Cam's barbershop on the east side waiting on him. Not seeing his car, I called him. He answered on the first ring.

"Where you at nigga, I'm out front?" I asked.

"We parked around back, pull around come through the back door," Darius told me.

I pulled the car around the back, and I saw my brother's car and two other cars. I hopped out and made my way to the back door. I walked in and saw my brother, Cam, and Clint sitting around the office.

"What it do y'all?" I spoke.

"Nothing much man, I can't call it," Clint said. Cam nodded, and Darius looked stressed out as hell.

"What's wrong, bruh? You didn't sound so good on the phone," I asked.

Finally, Darius spoke, "Man bruh, you need to check your bitch!"

"What?"

"You need to check your bitch!" Darius snapped with anger.

"Look I'm not gone take Ebony being called to many more bitches."

"Oh, she is gone be plenty more bitches once I tell you this shit," Darius said. This nigga was talking in circles.

"Nigga, what is it?"

"Dad's lawyer from the will, he would know all about any changes to the will, won't he?" Darius asked.

"Yeah, what the fuck is all this about?" I asked my brother.

"You might as well just start from the beginning, Darius," Cam jumped in.

I looked at Cam and back at my brother.

"Darius, what is going on?" I sighed.

"Your sweet little lady is playing you like a fiddle, well both of us. Do you know she went back and told Jamal everything that you had planned?" I rubbed my head looking confused.

"How you know all this?"

"Jazmine told me." Was he serious? I chuckled.

"Really, Jazmine of all people, didn't she steal from you?"

"That she did, but she stole from her own brother to pay me back all my money and more. Plus, she is carrying my child, but that's not all. How much do you really know about Ebony?" Darius asked.

I thought back to the phone call that I had gotten earlier from Jamal.

"I did get a phone call from that nigga Jamal at the office today. He told me anytime that I was ready for him just call. The only person knew what I was doing was Ebony, and when I called her to ask where she had been all day, she said she had seen Jamal, but she didn't know I had talked to him though. Why is she doing this?"

"I'm gone tell you why. Ebony was our pops little young thang. She was with pops before he got sick and shortly after before, he even told us. She got pregnant but pops made her get an abortion when he found out about Jamal. He then cut her ass out the will and left her. So, she called herself getting even by fucking around with us, trying to get back what she missed out on," Darius informed me.

My veins started to bulge out of the side of my neck. I jumped up.

"Wait, before you start going off, call the man that handled dad's will. Keep cool like ain't shit happened, like she did you. We will handle her after we handle Jamal's bitch ass. Speaking of which call that nigga and have him meet you on Cowan by the river at three a.m.," Darius instructed.

I nodded and called Jamal.

"Yeah?" he answered.

"If you don't want to go back to jail, meet me on Cowan Street under the bridge by the river at three a.m.," I ordered and hung up.

I stood to leave.

"I'll meet back up with you at three, I got to handle some shit," I said and walked out to leave.

Scrolling through my phone, I dialed the lawyer who had handled my father's will, which was a close friend of mine

"Hello, Aye Kirk. I need a huge favor. It's an emergency. I need any paperwork referring to my father's will, old wills, changes, etc. I need this like now and fax it to my home office," I ordered off. Kirk agreed with no questions asked.

I sped home hoping that Ebony was there. I shot her a text: *I MISS YOU. OMW HOME* I pressed send. I tossed the phone in the seat and continued to drive. I was thinking about everything my brother had said. I loved this girl, but she had fucked up beyond measures this time.

Pulling into the garage, I got out and hit the alarm. Walking at a fast pace to the elevators, I hit the floor to my condo. I stood in the elevator ready to bust through the doors. My patience was wearing very thin. Finally, the elevator stopped, and I got off and headed to my door.

As soon as I walked in, I headed straight to my office to grab the papers off the fax machine. Looking over the very first will my dad had, which had Darius and I listed as well as an Ebony Latrice Roseto receiving $50,000. The second will just has Darius and I listed on it. I grabbed the papers and barged out of my office looking for Ebony.

Ebony was sitting in bed watching TV.

"Hey, babe," she cooed when she saw me enter the room.

"What the fuck is this Ebony Roseto, I thought your name was Rose?" I asked, shoving the papers in Ebony's face.

Ebony grabbed the papers and scanned over them. She swallowed hard. Yep, her secret was out. She laid the papers down.

"I'm so sorry, Darnell," was all she could say.

"Sorry? Bitch, get your clothes on!" I yelled.

"Look, let's talk about this, Darnell. I really do love you." Ebony pleaded.

"Get your damn clothes on and let's go," I demanded.

Ebony got up and threw on some tights and a t-shirt as I stood there watching her get dressed with rage all over my face. When she was finished, I jacked her ass up by the arm and lead her out of the condo.

"Where are we going?" Ebony asked. I ignored her until we got in the car.

"Get in," I barked, shoving her in the car.

"Where does that nigga live at?"

"Who?" Ebony asked.

"Bitch, don't play with me. You know damn well who. The one you ran to today and told him all my damn business!" I yelled.

Ebony's eyes grew wide shocked that I knew what she did.

"He stays out north on 14th," Ebony panicked.

I put the car in drive and drove to Jamal's house.

Ebony

I was scared out of my damn mind. I didn't know what Darnell was capable of because he was pissed.

"What's the house number?" I heard Darnell ask.

"It's right there. The second house on the right." Darnell pulled up and placed the car in park.

"You gone take your ass up there and knock on the door, I'll be standing off to the side where he can't see me. When we get in this fucking house, you do as I say. Do you understand me?" he growled at me.

"Yeah," I replied.

We got out of the car and walked towards the front porch. Darnell stood to the right of the door while I beat on the door.

"Who the fuck is it?" Jamal yelled.

"It's me, Ebony." The door opened

"What are you doing here this late?" he asked.

"That nigga was tripping, so I had to leave. Can I come in?" I lied.

"Yeah," Jamal said, letting me in. As soon as he was about to close the door, Darnell rushed the door and hit Jamal with the butt of the gun he had.

"What the fuck?" Jamal yelled out in pain.

"Shut your ass up!" Darnell shouted. I covered my mouth crying. Darnell looked over at me.

"Shut up! Go find me something to tie his hands together and a pillowcase," he barked.

I did just that I ran off. When I got to the backroom, I pulled out my phone and press the voice recorder and place it in my bra. I grabbed a pillowcase and looked in the closet for something to tie Jamal's hands with. Not finding anything right away, I pulled some laces out of a pair of Jamal's shoes and ran back in the living room. Jamal was on the floor knocked out cold.

"What did you do?"

"I knocked his ass out. Give me that!" Darnell snapped reaching for the stuff. Darnell tied Jamal's wrist together. He pulled Jamal up and placed the pillowcase over his head.

"Get the door."

I ran to the door and opened it while Darnell dragged Jamal out of the house and placed him in the back seat. We hopped in the car and left like a thief in the night.

Darius

I was sitting on the hood of my car waiting for my brother to pull up. It was 3:20. When I called my brother, he didn't answer. Some lights caught my attention coming around the corner. Pulling in, I sat there and watched as he got out of the car. When the lights came on in the car, and I saw Ebony, I snapped.

"What the fuck is she doing here?" I said, walking towards the car.

"Chill out. I used her to get Jamal. Help me get this nigga out the car," Darnell said. When I looked in the back window, I saw Jamal laid out on the backseat.

"Still, this bitch is crooked, so this the last place she needs to be."

"Would you just help me get this nigga out the car, I'm not trying to be here all night." Darnell struggled, so I leaned in and helped to remove Jamal. This nigga was heavy as hell.

"Is he dead already?"

"No, I just knocked him out cold. I did this for you, so it's whatever you want to do, little bruh." Darnell said. We got to the edge of the embankment

"You go ahead and get out of here. I don't trust that bitch. I got it from here," I suggested.

"You sure?"

"Yeah, I'll hit you when I get home."

"Aite then," Darnell said and took off back towards the car.

Ebony

"Shit," I whispered as I hurried and put my phone up when I saw Darnell coming back towards the car. I had video recorded them carrying Jamal to the embankment.

Darnell got in the car and looked over at me.

"I should've thrown your ass in the river!" he spat.

I rolled my eyes then smirked. First thing in the morning I was taking this video and recordings to the police station.

Darius

Standing here with Jamal's ass, I didn't have much time, so I started to untie Jamal's wrist and took the pillowcase off his head. Jamal was still out cold, but I wanted this bitch ass nigga up so that he could know his fate. Lifting my leg, I kicked Jamal in the side.

"Get your ass up, nigga!" I spat. Jamal stirred barely opening his eyes.

"I just wanted you to see my face before I sent your ass to glory."

"Fuck you!" Jamal spat.

Pulling my gun out, I aimed it at Jamal. Right when I was about to shoot, I thought against it. I tucked the gun back in my waist and walked over to where I saw a brick. Picking it up, I hit Jamal twice in his head knocking him back out. I watched the blood roll out of Jamal's mouth. Not satisfied, I hit him again making sure that it was the blow that killed him. I threw the brick in the water and kicked Jamal with a push causing him to roll down the embankment into the Cumberland River. Standing there, I watched as his body got taken away by the current of the water.

Jazmine

Not hearing from Darius since we parted ways earlier today had me worried. Here it was going on 4:30 a.m. and still no word. There was no telling what Darius had done since he heard the news. When I heard the garage door opening, I let out a sigh of relief. Rushing to the door, I watched Darius get out the car.

"Where in the hell have you been, Darius? You had me fucking worried?" I asked. Darius looked up at me, and he didn't look like himself.

"I'm fine, but we need to talk," Darius mumbled.

When I gazed down at his shoes and noticed mud all over his shoes and his hands was bloody, I knew it was some shit in the game. I reached for his hands.

"Darius, what did you do?" I asked afraid of the outcome of the answer.

Darius walked into the laundry room. He washed his hands and then started removing his shirt and pants. He reached for some sweats and a wife beater. He was eerily quiet, and I watched him redress.

"Darius, talk to me?" I pleaded. Darius leaned up against the washer and sighed.

"Jazz, I killed your brother." He shrugged.

Darius looked at me as if he was trying to read me. I wasn't dumb, and I had figured that much out. When I came back to Darius that was a decision I had made, so I can see why he was wondering if I had changed my mind. Walking towards him, I caressed his face and leaned in and kissed him.

"You have nothing to say?" Darius asked.

"Do you think I didn't know the outcome of me telling you all that shit earlier? I'm fine, baby. You are my family," was my final say, and I leaned back in to continue kissing Darius.

Chapter 10

Darius

The next morning Jazmine and I laid in bed catching up on some much-needed rest. I looked over at her because that shit had been on my mind since yesterday,

"Ebony needs to be taken care of. Darnell brought her last night, and I don't trust that bitch." Jazmine frowned

"Why would he do that?" Jazmine asked.

"I don't even know. He claimed she helped him get your brother. She needs to be handled asap. If she was plotting before, this is the type of shit she likes."

"I never liked that bitch from the jump," Jazmine admitted.

"I need to call my brother and see what's up with her," I said reaching for the phone. I grabbed my phone and dialed him up. His phone rang three times before he answered,

"Yeah what's up?" he answered.

"What are we gone do about our little problem?"

"Well, right now her ass is locked up in my guest room, I could have her picked up for the murder charge that I got dropped for Jamal," Darnell said.

"Hell nah that shit is too easy. She's gone pay for all this damn shit she's caused!" I snapped.

"I'm gone handle it, Darius," Darnell said.

"Aite, keep me posted." I hung up the phone.

Ebony

When I heard the keys shuffling, I grew excited because Darnell had locked me in the room. I was fully dressed and sitting on the bed when he came in.

"Where do you think you're going?" he asked. I stood up.

"You are not about to keep me locked up in this room, Darnell. You can let me go. I'm not gone say anything, and you will never hear from me again."

"Girl, what makes you think I believe anything that comes out of your mouth. Sit tight. I'm gone hop in the shower, and I'll be back," Darnell said and walked out of the room, locking the door behind him again.

Shit, I was pissed because I needed to get to the police station. Walking over to the window, I took in the breathtaking view of the city. *I got to get the fuck out of here.* My phone beeped, and I looked down it was a text from my best friend, Kim.

"Kim, yes why didn't I think of this shit earlier," I said aloud. Instead of texting Kim back, I called her.

"Heffa you could've texted back instead of calling," Kim said.

"No, Kim I couldn't. I need a huge favor right now."

"Lord you and your favors." Kim sighed.

"Look, Darnell has me locked in a room, but I need you to take something to the police station for me."

"What, Ebony what the hell kind of freaky shit y'all on? Wait, did you say take something to the police station?" Kim asked.

"Look. I don't have time to go into details, but all I need you to do is come to Darnell's condo and tell him that you need your bag for work. Inside the bag will be my other phone and a note. All you have to do is take it to the precinct and drop it off to an officer," I quickly said.

"Ebony, you are scaring me," Kim said.

"Bitch, get it together. Are you coming or not?" I spat slightly irritated.

"Yeah, I'm on the way," Kim said and hung up the phone.

Darnell

After my shower, I found something to put on. I opted on some basketball shorts and a white tee, a pair of socks, and my Nike slides. I headed to the kitchen to fix me something to eat. I threw me a couple of slices of wheat bread in the toaster and placed two eggs in a pot to boil. I figured Ebony probably was hungry, so I walked to the room and unlocked the door.

"You can come out to fix you something to eat."

"Yessah Massah," Ebony said sarcastically.

I followed her back in the kitchen and started on my coffee. There was a knock on the door. I looked at Ebony.

"You better not move out this kitchen," I told her as I walked off to open the door.

When I opened the door my shit instantly got on brick from the beauty on the other side. I had seen Kim a couple of times but rarely paid her any attention, but damn she was beautiful.

"Oh, hey Kim," I said, looking Kim up and down. Kim licked her lips.

"You might want to fix that," Kim said, pointing down at my shorts. My shit was standing at attention.

"Is Ebony here? I um came to get my bag for work," Kim asked.

"Yeah, she's in the kitchen."

I stepped aside letting Kim in. I followed behind her walking into the kitchen to make sure Ebony kept her mouth shut.

"Let me get your bag," Ebony said walking off towards the room. My eyes started to roam over her body when Ebony walked out.

"You like what you see, Mr. Taylor?" Kim whispered. Right before I could answer, Ebony walked back in the kitchen with the bag

"Here you go, girl. You better get going. I don't want you late for work," Ebony said.

"Well yes, let me get going," Kim said.

"Nice seeing you, Darnell." She smiled.

"I'll let you out," Ebony said. I watched as Ebony walked Kim to the door.

Ebony walked back in the kitchen and crossed her arms giving me an ill look.

"What?" I asked.

"Don't think I didn't notice you flirting with my best friend. It's on full display," she said, pointing to my now semi hard-on. I looked down and chuckled, grabbing my dick.

"This isn't your concern no more, my girl. Now hurry and eat so that you can get back in the room."

Kim

That was some strange shit. I sat in the car wondering what the hell was in the bag that Ebony had given me. I opened the bag and pulled out the phone. I had no clue what I was looking for, but I was bound to find it. Ebony had deleted all her contacts, pictures, and everything except a video. I pressed play on the video, and my mouth dropped. I was in shock. Inside was an envelope as well. I removed the envelope out of the bag and opened it. It was Ebony's writing explaining how Darius and Darnell were planning to kill Jamal. It stated it was a recording in the phone also, so I went to the recordings and listened to the recording.

"What the hell has this bitch done got me involved in?" I mumbled. Placing the contents back in the bag, I headed to the police station.

Jasmine

Being pregnant, I had already picked up some bad habits. I was currently watching the news and eating my favorite ice cream. Darius was sitting next to me on a phone call. The news was talking about the drug overdoses in Tennessee surrounding the drug Fentanyl. That's when the perfect idea hit me. I set my bowl down on the table

"Babe," I nudged Darius.

Darius held up his finger and mouthed "Hold on."

I had thought of the perfect idea to handle little Miss Ebony. Darius finished up his phone call

"What's up girl, why you all antsy?" he asked.

"Could you get your hands on some Fentanyl?"

"Girl that Fentanyl shit will get a nigga locked up for real. Why are you asking about that shit?"

"I got a plan that might work and get Ebony out the picture. We can stage a suicide. All I need is a sample of her writing so that I can write a suicide note, and of course, Darnell needs to know about this so that we can plan a double date night at his place. While y'all are doing what y'all do in one room, I can give her the cocktail to drink and plant the pills— boom she's gone. She leaves the note, we find her, and call the police or whatever," I acted out.

I was serious, but Darius was cracking the hell up.

"You watch too much damn TV girl."

"You're laughing, but the shit can work. Hell, y'all ain't came up with nothing. Darnell is talking about sending her to jail, but what's that gone do? She still has a mouth and can talk whenever she gets ready."

"You do have a point. I'll think about it and run it across Darnell," Darius said.

Kim

I had been sitting outside the police station, and I was nervous as hell. I was contemplating whether to leave or take the bag in the precinct. I slowly got out of the car, looking around to see if anybody was watching me.

When I walked into, the station, I looked around, and panic kicked in. around

"I can't do this," I said to myself. I saw two cops in the hall talking.

"Fuck this," I mumbled, turning around to leave. That's when I heard the cops call out to me. Panicking, I bumped into another cop trying to leave out

"Oh, excuse me. I'm so sorry."

"Is everything ok, ma'am? the cop asked.

"I'm fine, thanks," I said, running to her car. I hopped in the car so fast and pulled off

"I don't know what Ebony got going on, but I've got to get this bag to Darnell," I said aloud.

Looking over to the passenger side seat, I didn't see the bag. I looked on the floorboard and back seat no bag.

"Fuck!" I yelled hitting the steering wheel.

"I must've dropped the bag when I bumped into that cop," I was scared shitless and was thinking how I could get in touch with Darnell.

***

Back at the station, the cop had picked up the bag that Kim had dropped.

"What was that all about?" another cop had walked up and asked.

"I have no clue. I'll handle it though." Officer Jordan said, heading into his office.

Closing the door behind him, he sat down at his desk. Opening the bag, he looked inside, and there was an envelope and a phone. Opening the envelope, he started to read the contents.

After reading the letter, he quickly retrieved the phone and looked at what was on the phone. He placed the phone and envelope back in the bag and pulled out his cellphone to make a call.

"Yeah, something has come up, and we need to meet asap. Ok. I'll meet you there in twenty minutes," Officer Jordan said and hung up the phone.

Chapter 11

Officer Jordan sat patiently waiting for his friend to arrive. He was sipping on a Red Bull waiting as time slowly crept by. When he saw his friend pull up, he did the same and started walking towards the building. Entering the building, he followed his friend into his office.

"Officer Jordan, what's up? I heard a little urgency in your voice," Darnell said.

"I think you may want to look at this." Officer Jordan said handing Darnell the bag he had gotten at the station. Darnell retrieved the bag and looked at the contents, his eyebrow furrowed.

"Where did you get this," Darnell asked.

"Some girl came to the station well she was running out the station she actually bumped into me, and she dropped a bag," Officer Jordan said.

"Do you know if she talked to anybody?" Darnell asked.

"I don't think so because Mike and Keith were in the hall, but they were trying to stop her also," Officer Jordan answered.

"They're cool. They're on payroll with me. The girl what did she look like?" Darnell asked.

"She was a bad little thang. She's light skin had golden blonde hair pulled up in a ponytail," Jordan described.

"Kim," Darnell said. Darnell stood up and walked over to his safe. He then pulled out some cash and handed it to Jordan.

"That's five grand. Thanks for bringing this directly to me." Darnell said.

"No problem D, you know we go way back." Officer Jordan said.

Officer Jordan left Darnell's office.

Darnell

At times like this, I was blessed as hell to have some of MNPD on my payroll. Yeah, I was a lawyer, but a nigga was raised by a thug and knew the streets well. Ebony was digging a bigger hole for herself. I placed everything in the safe and headed out. When I got home, Ebony ass had to be dealt with.

"Oh, thank god. I need to talk to you." Kim's voice caught me off guard. I looked at Kim.

"Ebony gave you that bag, didn't she?" I asked. Kim nodded her head

"Yes, and I think I dropped it at the station when I was trying to leave. I didn't want to go through with it, and I was gone bring it to you, but I didn't realize I had dropped it until after I pulled off. I knew I should've gone with my first instinct. I kept saying that I'm not finna get caught up for Ebony's ass."

Kim was just running off at the mouth she was a nervous wreck. I stepped forward and grabbed Kim.

"Would you calm down, girl. Luckily the officer that found the bag is on my payroll and brought it to me. One thing about me is I'm paying or helping half of MNPD out of their own legal troubles. I'm glad you thought against what your dumb ass homegirl was doing."

"I'm so sorry about everything that went down with y'all," Kim said sincerely.

"It just wasn't meant to be. She was playing a nigga from the start, but she got it coming." I nodded.

A nigga knew I was wrong for what I was about to do, but I couldn't resist. Leaning in, our lips met. I had never felt the electricity that shot through my body before from anybody. Kim broke our kiss.

"I'm sorry. I shouldn't have done that."

Placing my finger over her lips to silence her, I went back to kissing her. We kissed for what felt like an eternity. It was so wrong, but it felt so right.

Darius

Thanks to my white buddy I came across some Oxycodone pills laced with Fentanyl. I had gotten them just in case I took Jazmine up on her offer. I still wanted to talk to my brother though and run the idea past him. So, I dialed Darnell's number and let the phone ring.

"Man, I was just about to call you. Shit done got real," Darnell spoke into the phone.

"Aw hell, what done happened now?"

"Ebony's got to go asap. You know this bitch recorded every damn thing that we did the night things went down with Jamal and had Kim send that shit to the police. Kim freaked out dropping the bag trying to run and thank god Officer Jordan picked it up and brought it to me!" Darnell yelled.

"I told you shouldn't have brought her ass that night, but aye, Jazmine came up with a good idea. Come out to the crib so that I can break this shit down to you."

"Aite, on my way," Darnell said.

Darnell

When I got to my brother's house, just looking at the neighborhood had me ready to move.

"This makes a nigga want to move out here with the big dogs," I said. I rang the doorbell, and a young lady answered.

"You must be Jazmine?"

"The one and only," she said.

"Nice to finally meet you," I greeted her with a hug and walked into the house.

"Nice to meet you as well, Darius is down here. You can follow me." Jazmine said. I followed Jazmine downstairs to what was a theater room.

"Congrats on the baby."

"Thank you," Jazmine said, walking into the room.

Darius was laid back in one of the chairs watching *Deuces* on Netflix. I gave him dap and sat in the chair next to him.

"Can I get you anything?" Jazmine asked.

"Yeah, you can tell me about this idea you came up with for our little problem," I said, getting straight to the point.

Jazmine smirked and started telling me her idea. It was cool, and I could see us pulling it off.

"I think we could pull that off. What's better is we don't need no suicide note at all. We can just make it look like an overdose on her part. We don't want nothing coming back to any of us."

"I copped some of those Oxy pills today with the Fentanyl from my white home boy," Darius said, pulling out the bags from his pocket.

"Why is it in two bags?" Jazmine asked confused.

"So, nobody's prints are placed on the bag inside. Wear gloves when removing the bag or getting the pills out," Darius instructed.

I nodded in agreement.

"What does she like to drink, Darnell?" Jazmine asked

"Tequila."

"Cool. Darius, tomorrow just give me four pills out of there so that I can crush them down, I'll slip it in her drink while everybody is chilling. We can keep the remainder of the pills in the bag and plant it somewhere in the room she's in to make it look like she had a habit," Jazmine said.

We had come up with the perfect plan, and soon Ebony would be out the picture.

***

The next morning, I got up and cleaned the condo from top to bottom, bleaching everything down and doing the laundry. I even went into Ebony's room and cleaned up and washed the clothes and bed linens that she had in there.

"We are having company today, so you can come out because I need you to prepare something to eat for my brother and his girlfriend. She's pregnant so don't make shit too fucking spicy," I demanded.

Ebony turned her nose up.

"When did Darius get a girlfriend?" she asked.

The fuck she wanted to know for? I turned around and gave her a smug look

"You still worrying about shit that doesn't concern you. Why are you worried about my brother?" I asked, having flashbacks.

"Nothing Darnell, it was just a question," Ebony said.

"Anyway, I think you already know Jazmine. You know JAMAL's sister!" I spat and walked out of the room.

Jazmine

Trying my best not to wake Darius out of his sleep, I was hovered over the toilet throwing up its contents.

"You okay baby?" Darius asked, scaring me.

"Yes, this child is killing me with this damn nausea. Sorry, I woke you, babe," I said, wiping her mouth.

"It's all good. I'm just making sure you're straight."

I walked over to the sink and brushed my teeth. When I finished, I walked out of the bathroom

"What time are we heading over your brother's place?"

"Shit whenever, the quicker we do this shit, we can get on with our lives," Darius said.

Nodding my head, I went downstairs to the kitchen and retrieved two pairs of latex gloves and a face mask, which I put on immediately and grabbed a sandwich bag. Me being pregnant I didn't want my skin to come in contact or inhale anything dealing with Fentanyl.

Walking back in the bedroom I asked Darius, "Where them pills at?" He pointed to the nightstand.

"In the drawer."

I got the pills out of the drawer and went in the bathroom and removed four pills out the bag. I grabbed a glass and crushed the pills up as fine as I could and scooped the powder in the sandwich bag. When done I tied the bag and placed it in the other bag with the remainder of the pills. I walked back out the bathroom holding the bag in the air for Darius to see

"All done."

Ebony

This nigga got me up here slaving for motherfuckers who could give two shits about me. I made something quick and nothing fancy. He had me fucked up if he thought I was finna truly get down. Darnell walked in the kitchen and over to the stove

"Spaghetti!" He frowned.

"Yes, what's wrong with spaghetti?" I asked.

"Nothing," Darnell said. Darnell retrieved some plastic cups and set them on the countertop.

"Don't use any dishes tonight, all plastic please," he said.

Cool, I ain't want to be washing dishes anyway. I shrugged my shoulders, giving zero fucks about what Darnell said.

"My brother should be up any second. Act like you got some sense," Darnell said.

"Why should I? They asses don't like me. Why the hell are we doing this anyway?" I spat.

There was a knock on the door and Darnell went to answer.

"Hey y'all," he said, letting Darius and Jazmine in.

"What's up!" I heard them say.

They walked into the kitchen, and I was sitting there looking agitated as hell. Darius nodded, and Jazmine spoke.

"Hey Ebony, it's been a minute since I last saw you," Jazmine said. I chuckled.

"Hello, Jazmine. Sorry to hear about your brother," I said sarcastically. Jazmine smiled as if she knew I was fucking with her.

"Thanks, I heard you like Tequila," Jazmine said holding up the Patrón bottle they had bought.

"That I do, and I most definitely need a drink," I snatched the bottle from Jazmine and grabbed a plastic cup to pour me a shot. I walked into the living room to sit down, and Darius and Darnell followed.

Jazmine

This hoe was being funny about my brother, but now I was about to have the last laugh. Reaching down into my purse, I grabbed the gloves and put them on, and then I pulled out the plastic bag that contained the Fentanyl powder. My adrenaline was running like a motherfucker at the excitement of killing this bitch, so I decided to crush up two more pills with the four I already had. I then placed the powder in the cup and poured some Patrón in and added some ice along with pineapple juice giving it a nice stir.

"Don't mind me y'all. I'm fixing me a plate of spaghetti. Y'all know I got to eat," I called out to buy her some time. After a few minutes, I walked out of the kitchen and handed Ebony a cup

"I figured since you downed that shot, you were ready for another round." I smiled.

"Thanks, girl. You're not so bad after all," Ebony said.

I sat down and started to feed my face. Darius and Darnell were engaged in small talk while I watched Ebony sip on her drink. Once I was done, I headed back in the kitchen to throw my stuff away. I grabbed the Patrón bottle and took it back in the living room.

"Ebony, girl, where is y'all bathroom? This baby got me going every five minutes," I asked.

"It's one down the hall on the right," Ebony pointed.

As I walked down the hall, I spotted the bathroom, but it was the bedroom Ebony had been staying in that I was looking for. When I found the room, I put my gloves back on and pulled the pills out of her pocket, placing them in the nightstand.

Ebony

I'm not sure how much Patrón I had, but baby it seems to be taking over my body. My vision started to blur, and my heart felt like it was about to pop out my chest. The massive headache that followed was painful as hell. I could see everyone in the living room lips moving sounding like a bunch of gibberish. I rubbed my forehead, feeling the sweat run down my face and I felt a touch on my knee

"Ebony, are you ok?" Darnell asked.

Shaking my head, I managed to get out a few words.

"I'm gone go lay down, I don't feel good," I slurred.

Slowly I stood and walked to the room. There was a bottle of water on the nightstand that I had sitting there, so I took a sip and opened the drawer looking for some Tylenol, I saw a bag of pills that looked like ibuprofen. Opening the bag, I removed two pills flushing them down with water.

***

I was woken up out my sleep by convulsions. I couldn't control my body, and my mouth started foaming. The next thing I know, I was on the floor.

Darnell

"What was that?" I asked after hearing a loud noise come from the back. We all hopped up and ran in the room where Ebony was. Ebony was laid out on the floor, I bent down and checked Ebony's pulse

"Is she dead?" Jazmine asked.

I nodded.

"Jazmine, you make the call and sound all frantic and shit," Darius instructed. Jazmine did as she was told, placing the phone on speaker.

"911, what's your emergency?" the operator said.

"Oh, my god, we need an ambulance!" Jazmine cried into the phone.

"Ok ma'am, what seems to be the problem?" the operator asked.

"I don't know. My friend said she had a headache and came and laid down. I then heard a loud thump and came in the room she was foaming at the mouth," Jazmine cried.

"What's your address, ma'am?" the operator asked.

"We're at the Adelicia Condos downtown, apartment 1114. Darnell, what's the numeric address?" Jazmine asked.

"900 20th Avenue South."

"900 20th Avenue South Apt 1114," Jazmine told the operator.

"Ok ma'am, just stay calm. An ambulance is on its way," the operator said.

"Thank you," Jazmine said and hung up the phone.

When she got off the phone, we all stood and looked at Ebony's body not saying a word to each other. Jazmine had a smirk on her face extremely proud of her work.

About ten minutes later the paramedics and police arrived. Two cops were talking to Darius and Jazmine, and one was talking to me. The paramedics carried Ebony out in a body bag. An officer came out of the bedroom carrying the pills and a card. He approached me.

"We found this card in her nightstand along with the pills." I looked at Jazmine.

"What?" Jazmine said walking towards the officer and me. The officer showed her the card.

"Do you know a Jamal?" he asked.

"Yes, that's my brother," Jazmine said.

"This card had a number and his name along with "Pill man" beside it. We assume this is who she purchased the pills from," the officer said.

"I haven't spoken to my brother in a couple of days," Jazmine answered.

"Do y'all have any idea why she was taking these or why she possibly wanted to kill herself?" the officer asked.

I then spoke up.

"No sir, I know she had been having headaches a lot, but this doesn't seem like something that she would do. Jamal and her used to be involved a long time ago, but I wasn't aware they were even still communicating."

"Ok well, we're going to wrap things up here and get out of you all hair. This looks to be an apparent suicide, Mr. Taylor I'm sorry for your loss," the officer said.

"Thank you. Can I talk to you privately for a second, officer?"

"Sure," the officer said.

"I don't want this released to the media. I don't need this kind of publicity right now. Make sure you tell the medics and whoever you need to tell. I got you covered when your shift ends. Just call me."

"No problem, Mr. Taylor, anything you say. I don't want the chief biting my head off for not respecting your wishes," the officer said.

"Thank you."

The condo was finally cleared of officers and people running in and out. Darius and Jazmine were sitting in the living room. I walked into the kitchen and poured me a drink. I took a sip of the Patrón, and the warm liquid was soothing. I then walked into the living room

"Jazmine, good looking on that whole damn plan, I take it you planted the card also with Jamal's name?" I asked.

Jazmine nodded and smiled

"I just threw a little distraction in there to make them think they needed to find Jamal and not look at us," Jazmine said.

"Yeah, when he came out asking about Jamal, I figured it was some shit, but that was a good idea."

Darius stood up and grabbed Jazmine's hand.

"Girl, you just don't know how much I truly appreciate you. You've done some shit over these last couple of days that I would have never imagined. You make the perfect little ride or die," Darius said, kissing Jazmine.

I rolled my eyes.

"Ok, y'all two lovebirds need to take that mess on home. I must do my part and contact Ebony's mom and throw her ass some money for Ebony's burial expenses or whatever she wants to do with it. I got to play this thing out like the loving boyfriend I'm supposed to be." I sighed.

Darius nodded in agreeance and walked over to me.

"Aite then, you take care of that and call me if you need anything. We gone head on out. I love you, bruh," Darius said.

"I love you too, nigga," I said, pulling him in for a hug. Jazmine also hugged me.

When I was all alone, I walked back to the guest room where Ebony had died and stood there staring into space. My mind flashed back to the good times we had but was quickly overshadowed by all the fucked-up things she had done or set out to do. The thoughts had caused me to get angry all over again.

Walking out, I closed the door to the room pulling out my cell phone, I placed a call to my home girl's cleaning services, Immaculate Queens, to come out and clean the room right away. Thank god for hardwood floors, but I didn't want to deal with anything else regarding Ebony. After doing my part by contacting her mother and giving her some money, I was finally finna be done with Ebony Rose, well Ebony Roseto.

Epilogue

Darnell

A year had passed, and everything was finally back to normal. Business was still business for my firm, and I was set to open another firm in Memphis. After Ebony's death, shit was crazy, but I started dating her friend Kim. We couldn't help the attraction we had for one another. I was hesitant at first, but she was the complete opposite of Ebony. The best thing about her was I knew for a fact that she was the one I was going to marry one day.

Ebony's death investigation was ruled as a suicide. Ebony's mom had Ebony cremated so that she could pocket most the money I had given her.

About two months after Ebony's death, a fisherman discovered Jamal's badly decayed body while fishing. His death remains unsolved.

Darius and Jazmine welcomed a baby boy. Darius was more behind the scenes since the birth of his son. He had invested in some businesses thanks to his homie Cam, and his biggest investment was becoming part owner in my firm and helping to open the new Taylor & Miles in Memphis, TN.

Jazmine never brought up the things she did for us. I think it was a part of her that she buried away. When Jamal's body was found, she, along with her mom, had to identify what was left of him. Maybe one day she will feel bad for the betrayal against her brother, but until that day, it was just a distant memory.

Here we were standing at our father's grave silently taking in the feeling. This was our first time coming out here since the passing of our dad.

"Man pops, you left a helluva mess here for us to clean up. Thankfully, it was nothing that we couldn't handle together as brothers. I guess you bringing us together was cool after all."

Darius laughed trying to hide the fact that he was really choked up. I placed my hand on his back to let him know that it was ok to cry, so he finally let them fall. Darius then wiped his tears and continued talking. "Old Ebony was trying to take us down. I guess you pissed her off. You got a grandson now too, another generation of Miles for you."

I placed some flowers on the grave.

"You would be so proud of us, old man. Now that everything is back to normal, we will come out here once a month, have a few beers, and talk it up like old times," I said thinking back to times when my father and I would hang out.

"Love you, pops," I said.

Darius touched the headstone and whispered, "I love you."

We both turned around and walked back to the car.

"That wasn't as bad as I thought it was gone be," Darius said.

I nodded and patted my brother on the back.

"How did it go?" Kim asked. She and Jazmine were waiting outside the car while we visited our father.

"It was cool," I told her as we embraced.

Darius reached for his son who was in Jazmine's arms.

"Yeah, it was cool. I wish my little man here got to meet his granddad. He would've been spoiled rotten," Darius said. He leaned in and kissed Jazmine. We all laughed.

At this exact moment, life was great. Everyone was happy, but how long will this peace last because it's always some mess in the city.

The End

Thank you

Thank you so much for reading. Please leave a review good or bad. Once again both of the stories in this book were re-releases of my earlier work that I had self-published when I first came out in 2017. If you had read any of my book in my catalog you can see my growth as a writer. Thanks for the continued support.

My Catalog

A Savage and his Lady 1 & 2 (Series)

Masking My Pain

Fiyah & Desire: Down to ride for a Boss

Securing the Bag and His Heart (Series)

Securing the Bag and His Heart Too

Remnants (Novella)

5 Miles Until Empty (Novella)

Once Upon a Hood Love: A Nashville Fairytale (Novella)

Tricked: A Halloween Love Story (Novella)

Kali Kusain: Counterfeit Queen (Standalone)

Dear Saint Nik: A Christmas (Novella)

My First Night with You: a BWWM (Novella)

Enticed by a Cold Hearted Menace (Standalone)

CPSIA information can be obtained
at www.ICGtesting.com
Printed in the USA
LVHW090309121019
633942LV00001BA/98/P